First World War
and Army of Occupation
War Diary
France, Belgium and Germany

61 DIVISION
183 Infantry Brigade
Gloucestershire Regiment
2/4th (City of Bristol) Battalion, Territorial
1 September 1915 - 22 December 1917

WO95/3060/1

The Naval & Military Press Ltd
www.nmarchive.com
Published in association with The National Archives

Published by

The Naval & Military Press Ltd

Unit 10 Ridgewood Industrial Park,

Uckfield, East Sussex,

TN22 5QE England

Tel: +44 (0) 1825 749494

www.naval-military-press.com

www.nmarchive.com

This diary has been reprinted in facsimile from the original. Any imperfections are inevitably reproduced and the quality may fall short of modern type and cartographic standards.

© **Crown Copyright**
Images reproduced by permission of The National Archives, London, England, 2015.

Contents

Document type	Place/Title	Date From	Date To
Heading	61 Div 183 1.b. 2-4 Bn. Glosters Sep 1915-Feb 1918		
Heading	61st Division 183rd Infy Bde 2-4th Bn Glosters. 1915 Sep-1918 Feb (1916 Feb Mar Air Diaries Missing)		
Miscellaneous	War Diary Summary 2/4 Division Reg. Aug 31st 1915 Epping	03/09/1915	03/09/1915
War Diary	Epping	01/09/1915	30/09/1915
War Diary	Brentwood Essex	31/10/1915	31/10/1915
War Diary	Brentwood	01/12/1915	01/12/1915
Heading	War Diary Of 2/4 Gloster Reg. From 1st-Dec. 15 & 31st Dec 1915		
War Diary	Brentwood	01/12/1915	31/12/1915
Heading	War Diary Of 2/4 Bad Gloster Reg From 1st Jan 1916-31 Jan 1916		
War Diary	Brentwood	01/01/1916	31/01/1916
Operation(al) Order(s)	2/4th Battalion Gloucester Regt. Operation Orders. No. 37.	13/01/1916	13/01/1916
Operation(al) Order(s)	Operation Orders No 10		
Operation(al) Order(s)	Operation Orders No 14 By Lt Col C Pierce	26/01/1916	26/01/1916
Miscellaneous	61 Division 183 Infantry Brigade 2/4 Batt G Louestershire Reg Feb Mar April 1916 Missing		
Heading	2/4th Gloucester Regiment 23rd To 31st May 1916		
War Diary	Tidworth	23/05/1916	23/05/1916
War Diary	Southampton	24/05/1916	24/05/1916
War Diary	Havre	25/05/1916	31/05/1916
Map	La Pierriere		
Miscellaneous	2/4th Bn. Gloster Regt. Battalion Orders.		
Miscellaneous	Appendix		
Miscellaneous	2/4th Bn. Gloster Regt. Battalion Orders.		
Miscellaneous	Casualties Since leaving Tidworth Appendix 4		
Heading	War Diary Of 2/4th Batt Gloucestershire Regiment From June 1st 1916 To June 30th 1916 Volume I		
War Diary	Les Lobes	01/06/1916	01/06/1916
War Diary	In Liehert Sec	02/06/1916	09/06/1916
War Diary	Les Lobes	10/06/1916	10/06/1916
War Diary	Riez Bailleul	11/06/1916	16/06/1916
War Diary	A2.a. M28d55	17/06/1916	18/06/1916
War Diary	Near Line Edenden Home 19 35d 68 To M 29d 108	19/06/1916	21/06/1916
War Diary	Riez Bailleul M.7.d.	22/06/1916	30/06/1916
Operation(al) Order(s)	2/4th Bn. Gloster Regt. Operation Orders. No. 6.	10/06/1916	10/06/1916
Miscellaneous	2/4th Bn. Gloster Regt. Appendix.		
Miscellaneous	2/4th Battalion Gloucestershire Regiment. Battalion Orders. No. 15 Appendix 2	20/06/1916	20/06/1916
Miscellaneous	2/4th Battalion Gloucestershire Regiment. Casualties For Month Ending June 30th 1916	30/06/1916	30/06/1916
Heading	War Diary Of 2/4th Battalion Gloucestershire Regt From 1st July 1916 To 31st July 1916 Volume 3		
War Diary	Riez Bailleul	01/07/1916	03/07/1916
War Diary	Front-Pauquissart Sub-Secn	04/07/1916	08/07/1916
War Diary	Fruquissart Sub-Seon	09/07/1916	09/07/1916
War Diary	Laventie	09/07/1916	14/07/1916

War Diary	Fauquissart Sub-Secn	15/07/1916	20/07/1916
War Diary	Estaires	21/07/1916	23/07/1916
War Diary	Levantie	24/07/1916	25/07/1916
War Diary	Fauquissant Sub-Secn	26/07/1916	31/07/1916
Miscellaneous	183 Brigade Appendix A	05/07/1916	05/07/1916
Miscellaneous	The O.C. C. Coy.		
Miscellaneous	183rd Inf Bde.	20/07/1916	20/07/1916
Miscellaneous	A Form. Messages And Signals.	04/09/1916	04/09/1916
Miscellaneous	C Form (Duplicate). Messages And Signals.	06/07/1916	06/07/1916
Diagram etc			
Miscellaneous	Dear Tupman	05/07/1916	05/07/1916
Miscellaneous	G.O.C. 183 Inf. Bde.	05/07/1916	05/07/1916
Miscellaneous	183 Brigade.	05/07/1916	05/07/1916
Miscellaneous	D.A.G., 3rd Echelon, Base	05/09/1916	05/09/1916
Miscellaneous	The O C 2/4th Gloster	08/07/1916	08/07/1916
Miscellaneous	The O.C. 2/4 Gloucesters	08/07/1916	08/07/1916
Miscellaneous	A Form. Messages And Signals.	12/07/1916	12/07/1916
Miscellaneous	2/4 Gloster 2/7 Worcesters	13/07/1916	13/07/1916
Miscellaneous	Division Routine Orders By Major General Colin Mackenzie C.B. Commanding 61st Division.	29/07/1916	29/07/1916
Miscellaneous	Notes For C Coy		
Diagram etc			
Heading	War Diary Of 2/4th Battalion Gloucestershire Regiment. From 1st August 1916 To 31st August 1916. Volume I		
War Diary	Fauquissart (Left Sub Secn)	01/08/1916	01/08/1916
War Diary	Laventie	02/08/1916	05/08/1916
War Diary	Fauquissart (Left Sub-Secn)	06/08/1916	09/08/1916
War Diary	La Gorgue	09/08/1916	17/08/1916
War Diary	Croix Barbee (Neuve Chapelle Section)	18/08/1916	18/08/1916
War Diary	Croix-Barbee	19/08/1916	21/08/1916
War Diary	Neuve Chap NE Left Sub Section	22/08/1919	26/08/1919
War Diary	Riez Bailleul	26/08/1918	31/08/1918
Heading	War Diary Of 2/4th Battalion Gloucestershire Regiment From 1st September 1916 To 30th September 1916 Volume 5		
War Diary	Moated Grange Secn	01/09/1916	07/09/1916
War Diary	Riez Bailleul	07/09/1916	10/09/1916
War Diary	Robermetz	11/09/1916	15/09/1916
War Diary	Boutdeville	16/09/1916	19/09/1916
War Diary	Neuve Chapelle Section	20/09/1916	26/09/1916
War Diary	Boutdeville	27/09/1916	30/09/1916
Miscellaneous	O.C.C. 2/4th Gloucester Regt	24/09/1916	24/09/1916
Miscellaneous	2/4 Gloucester Regt	24/09/1916	24/09/1916
Miscellaneous	183rd Bde.	24/09/1916	24/09/1916
Miscellaneous	2/4th Gloucester Regt	25/09/1916	25/09/1916
Miscellaneous	Code	25/09/1916	25/09/1916
Miscellaneous	No 2 Field Of R.E.	25/09/1916	25/09/1916
Miscellaneous	C Form (Duplicate). Messages And Signals.	25/09/1916	25/09/1916
Miscellaneous	Very Secret	25/09/1916	25/09/1916
Miscellaneous	O.C. 4th Glosters	25/09/1916	25/09/1916
Diagram etc	25/9/16 Barrage If Required		
Miscellaneous	C Form (Duplicate) Messages And Signals.	27/07/1916	27/07/1916
Heading	War Diary Of 2/4th Battalion Gloucestershire Regt From October 1st 1916 To October 31st 1916 Volume 5		
War Diary	Bout De Ville	01/10/1916	31/10/1916

Heading	War Diary Of 2/4th Batt Glos. Regt. from Nov. 1st 1916 To Nov. 30th 1916		
War Diary	In The Field	01/11/1916	30/11/1916
Heading	War Diary 2/4 Glosters. December 1916		
Heading	War Diary. Vol. 8 Of The 2/4 Batt. The Gloucestershire Reg. December 1916.		
War Diary		01/12/1916	31/12/1916
Heading	War Diary. Of The 2nd 4th. Bn. The Gloucestershire Regiment. Vol. 9 January 1917.		
War Diary		01/01/1917	31/01/1917
Heading	War Diary Of The 2/4th Bn. Gloucestershire Regiment Vol. 10.		
War Diary		01/02/1916	28/02/1916
Heading	War Diary Of The 2/4th Battalion Gloucestershire Regt Vol. II.		
War Diary		01/03/1916	31/03/1916
Heading	War Diary Of The 2/4th Battalion. The Gloucestershire Regiment. Vol 12		
War Diary		01/04/1916	30/04/1916
Miscellaneous	2/4th Bn Gloucestershire Regt		
Heading	2/4th Bn. Gloucestershire Regt. War Diary. Volume 13 May. 1917.		
War Diary	Germaine	01/05/1917	31/05/1917
Miscellaneous	2/4 Bn Gloucestershire Regiment Appendix "B" To War Diary		
Map			
Miscellaneous	Report ?		
Heading	2/4th Battn. Gloucestershire Regiment. War Diary June 1917. Volume 14		
War Diary	Dainville	01/06/1917	30/06/1917
Miscellaneous	2/4th Bn Gloucestershire Regiment Appendix "A" To War Diary.		
Heading	2/4th Battn Gloucestershire Regt. War Diary. Volume 15 July. 1917		
War Diary	Fillievres	01/07/1917	31/07/1917
Miscellaneous	2/4th Batt. Gloucestershire Regiment. Appendix "A" To War Diary.		
Heading	2/4th Bn. Gloucestershire Regt. War Diary. Volume 16 August 1917		
War Diary	Nieuland	01/08/1917	31/08/1917
Map			
Miscellaneous	Message Form.		
Miscellaneous	2/4th Bn Gloucestershire Regiment.		
Map			
Heading	War Diary 2/4th Battn Gloucestershire Regt Sept. 1917 Vol. 18		
War Diary	Brandhoek	01/09/1917	30/09/1917
Miscellaneous	Appendix. B. Report On Operations Aug 27th 1917	27/08/1917	27/08/1917
Miscellaneous	2/4th Bn Gloucestershire Regiment. Appendix "A" To War Diary		
Heading	2/4th Batt. The Gloucestershire Regiment War Diary Vol. 18. October 1917.		
War Diary		01/10/1917	31/10/1917
Miscellaneous	2/4th Bn Gloucestershire Regiment. Appendix To War Diary. October 1917.		
Miscellaneous		24/10/1917	24/10/1917

Miscellaneous	2/4th Battalion Gloucestershire Regiment	24/10/1917	24/10/1917
Operation(al) Order(s)	2/4th Battalion Gloucestershire Regiment. Operation Orders No. 91	23/10/1917	23/10/1917
Heading	2/4th. Bn Gloucestershire Regiment War Diary. Volume 19. November 1917		
War Diary		01/11/1917	30/11/1917
Heading	2/4th Battn The Gloucestershire Regiment. War Diary. Vol. 20. December. 1917.		
War Diary	Havrincourt Wood	01/12/1917	31/12/1917
Miscellaneous	2/4th Battalion Gloucestershire Regt. Operation Orders No 100	09/12/1917	09/12/1917
Operation(al) Order(s)	2/4th Battalion Gloucestershire Regt. Operation Orders No 101	15/12/1917	15/12/1917
Operation(al) Order(s)	2/4th Battalion Gloucestershire Regiment. Operation Orders No 102	19/12/1917	19/12/1917
Operation(al) Order(s)	2/4th Battalion Gloucestershire Regt. Operation Orders No 103	22/12/1917	22/12/1917
Miscellaneous	2/4th Bn Gloster Regt	22/12/1917	22/12/1917
War Diary	Addendum To O/O No 104	22/12/1917	22/12/1917
Operation(al) Order(s)	2/4th Battalion Gloucestershire Regiment. Operation Orders No. 105	23/12/1917	23/12/1917
Operation(al) Order(s)	2/4th Battalion Gloucestershire Regiment. Operation Orders No. 106.	30/12/1917	30/12/1917
Miscellaneous	Table A First Train Starting 1 Pm. From Etricourt Stn.		
Miscellaneous	Table B. Third (Omnibus) Train Starting At 8 Pm. From Ytres Stn		

2-4 BN. GLOSTERS
61 DIV, 1B,
183,
SEP 1915 — FEB 198

61ST DIVISION
183RD INFY BDE

2-4TH BN GLOSTERS.
~~MAY 1916 - FEB 1918~~

1915 SEP — ~~1916 JAN~~
~~1916 MAY~~ — 1918 FEB
(1916 FEB, MAR, APR DIARIES MISSING)

DISBANDED

War Diary Summary
2/4 Gloster. Reg. Aug 31st 1915. Epping.

Training During this period the Bat. has paraded under Senior Company Officers in rotation, carrying out a course of trench digging on a field adjoining The Fords Danbury which has been very instructive as the work was rendered difficult on account of so much rain which caused the flooding of the trenches & in many places falls. Aug 24–26 each half Bat. occupied the trenches at Maldon for 24 hours.
Several very instructive lectures were given including.
Aug 9. Lecture at Ipswich on trench warfare to Officers & NCO's by Col Burrows
Aug 10. Lecture at Chelmsford on lessons learnt in tactical handling of M.G's in the present war by Capt Lindsay
Aug 11. Staff lecture by Capt Davis on outpost scheme on the ground already selected by syndicates.
Aug 26 Lecture at Maldon by Mr Gordon on mapreading etc
     27   "   " Danbury "   "   "   "   "   "
The Bat took part in three inspections as follows:—
Aug 4 Brig. was inspected by Brig Gen. The Marquis of Salisbury at Woodham Mortimer Rifle Range
Aug 6 Div was inspected by Field Marshal Earl Kitchener K.G. GCB. OM. GCSI. GCIE at Hylands Park.
Aug 27. ½ Bat was inspected by Gen Inglis in trenches at Maldon.
Aug 30 The Bat marched to Epping leaving Danbury at 5 am & reaching camp at 5pm. without any man falling out.
Aug 19. The Bat took part in Brig concentration march to Cold Norton

Recruiting 39 men were received from 3/4 Gloster Malvern Wells on Aug 9
Transport Aug 7. 11 large draft mules were received.

S Shelland Major

Gloster's

2/4 GLOSTER REGT

Army Form C. 2118

WAR DIARY
or
INTELLIGENCE SUMMARY.
(Erase heading not required.)

Hour, Date, Place	Summary of Events and Information	Remarks and references to Appendices
Epping Sept 1–30 1915 2/4 Gloster Reg.	During this period the Bat. has been under Canvas at Epping & have been engaged in Bat. field training three days & Bri. training three days weekly. Sept 10th The G.O.C. The Marquis of Salisbury inspected the camp. " 11th Incendiary & explosive bombs were dropped in & near the 6th Gloster camp by the enemies aircraft but no damage was done. The recruits have been trained separately & have been put thro' a course of musketry on the miniature range. Recruiting – Sept 4th 5 men were received from Clacton.	Shelland Major.

Confidential

Army Form C. 2118.

WAR DIARY
—or—
INTELLIGENCE SUMMARY. ¾ Glostr Reg

(Erase heading not required.)

Instructions regarding War Diaries and Intelligence Summaries are contained in F.S. Regs., Part II. and the Staff Manual respectively. Title pages will be prepared in manuscript.

Hour, Date, Place	Summary of Events and Information	Remarks and references to Appendices

Brentwood, Essex
 	
Oct 31st 1915
	During this period up to the 25th inst the Bat continued Bat 3 days Bn 2 days Bn training 1 day each week including 4 days 11" to 15" inst on manoeuvres to Blackmore & Hatfield Peverel. On the 25th inst the Bat marched into C. Bn. into Brentwood when the troops were billeted, the remainder of the period being utilized for company work & one Bn day.
	
	Recruits continued numerically at Epping & company work at Brentwood & were carried on through a the marches large
	
	No recruits received
	
	No drafts sent away
	
	                Shelland
	                 Major
		[Stamp: 3/4 BN. GLOSTER REGT
		ORDERLY ROOM
		No. CR80
		Date 31/10/15]

Nov 15

CONFIDENTIAL

Army Form C. 2118.

WAR DIARY
INTELLIGENCE SUMMARY. 2/4 Glosh Reg.
(Erase heading not required.)

Instructions regarding War Diaries and Intelligence Summaries are contained in F.S. Regs., Part II. and the Staff Manual respectively. Title pages will be prepared in manuscript.

[Stamp: 2/1/4th BN. GLOSTER REGT. No. CR83 Date 3/12/15 ORDERLY ROOM]

Hour, Date, Place	Summary of Events and Information	Remarks and references to Appendices
Brentwood. Dec 1st 1915	During the period extra bombing, machine gun & signalling sections having been selected from the Battalion for special training under ditto officers special attention has been paid to bayonet fighting. The remainder of the Bat. has continued company training under Coy. Officers. All Japanese rifles have been returned & substituted by 303. Musketry ranges has been made at which companies in rotation are doing a course under the M.O. 8 Officers were returned to the 3rd Line on Nov 25th.	

Stewart
Major.

Confidential

War Diary of
7th Gurkha Reg.

from 1st Dec. 15 to 31st Dec 1915

Army Form C. 2118.

WAR DIARY
of
INTELLIGENCE SUMMARY.
(Erase heading not required.) 1/6 Gloster Reg

Instructions regarding War Diaries and Intelligence Summaries are contained in F.S. Regs., Part II and the Staff Manual respectively. Title pages will be prepared in manuscript.

Hour, Date, Place		Summary of Events and Information	Remarks and references to Appendices
1.12.15	BRENTWOOD	525 .303 rifles+bayonets received from WEEDON. 9 Sergeants transferred to E.F.	85.
2.12.15	"	Company training. Musketry range practise daily for companies & details as written.	85.
3.12.15	"	Batt. marched to MOUNT NESSING which dying under MAJOR GWYNN	85.
4.12.15	"	8.45am Batt. marched via BROOK. ST. HARROD WOOD. REDDEN COURT Gt WARLEY. INGRAVE GREEN under MAJOR SHELLARD	85.
5.12.15	"	Redistribution of Officers to various companies. Church parade 8.40am	85.
6.12.15	"	Bayonet fighting class under Sgt Eschinow daily 9.15am to 10.15am & 2.30pm to 3.30pm	85.
7.12.15	"	6 Light draft mules sent to Gt BADDOW	85.
8.12.15	"	Company training	85.
9.12.15	"	Majors Yeats Brown & Grant Crawley were attached to WITHAM following attached to this company viz: Captains Grant Weddey Staffs Ireland & Cpl Pumbley - Thomas	85.
10.12.15	"	Batt. marched 7.45 at 9am to MT NESSING bivouac'd all night	85.
11.12.15	"	4 light draft mules sent to R.E. WITHAM	85.
12.12.15	"	Church Parade 8.40am	85.
13.12.15	"	Sgt Eschinow reported to Chelsea	85.
14.12.15	"	Company training	85.
15.12.15	"	9 horses draft horses received. GOC Marquis of Salisbury inspected Coy. dining rooms	85.
16.12.15	"	Company training	85.
17.12.15	"	" "	85.
18.12.15	"	Brigade route march via INGRAVES. EAST. HOUNDON STATION. CHIRDERDITCH. BRENTWOOD.	85.
19.12.15	"	Church Parade 8.40am	85.
20.12.15	"	Company training	85.
21.12.15	"	do	85.
22.12.15	"	2 Bar - Shinal no 2 range tubes received	85.
23.12.15	"	Company training	85.
24.12.15	"	GOC Major Gen. R Baumaline Allison visited the Batt.	85.

Army Form C. 2118.

WAR DIARY
or
INTELLIGENCE SUMMARY.   2/4 Gloster Regt.
(Erase heading not required.)

Instructions regarding War Diaries and Intelligence Summaries are contained in F.S. Regs., Part II. and the Staff Manual respectively. Title pages will be prepared in manuscript.

Hour, Date, Place	Summary of Events and Information	Remarks and references to Appendices
25.12.15 BRENTWOOD	Church parade 8.45 am	85.
26.12.15 "	" 8.40 "	85.
27.12.15 "	Instruction in Bom - Short range firing for 2 weeks to A-B Coys by 2/Lt Huppert-James.	85.
28.12.15 "	9 new G.S. limber wagons received. 9 P.S. wagons handed over to 3 Coy. A.S.C.	85.
29.12.15 "	Company training	85.
30.12.15 "	Lt Col Rieu proceeded on leave. Major Shekell assumed command of Lt. Bat.	85.
31.12.15 "	Sniping class commenced under Lt James.	85.

Shekell Major
2/4 Gloster Regt.

[signature] Th Rieu
Lt. Col.
Comdg. 2/4th Bn. Gloucester Regt.

Confidential

War Diary of

1st Bn Leicester Regt

from 1st Jan 1916 — 31 Jan 1916

Army Form C. 2118.

WAR DIARY
or
INTELLIGENCE SUMMARY.
(Erase heading not required.)

Instructions regarding War Diaries and Intelligence Summaries are contained in F.S. Regs., Part II. and the Staff Manual respectively. Title pages will be prepared in manuscript.

Stamp: 2/5TH BN GLOUCR REGT. No. CR.10.6 Date 1/2/16 ORDERLY ROOM

Hour, Date, Place	Summary of Events and Information	Remarks and references to Appendices
Brentford		
1/1/16	Reg Exercise under CAPT LEDWARD	S.S.
2/1/16	Church Parade 9.40 am	S.S.
3/1/16	Company Training. Musketry range companies in Athletics under M.O.	S.S.
4/1/16	Company training. Board of survey assembled to Company equipment clothing will the clothing Experts.	S.S.
5/1/16	Company training	S.S.
6/1/16	"	S.S.
7/1/16	"	S.S.
8/1/16	Reg Exercise under LT PRATT Bat marched 17th 9.0 am via GT WARLEY, CROUCHERS. PUDDLE DOCK. WARLEY BARRACKS.	S.S.
9/1/16	Church Parade 8.40 am.	S.S.
10/1/16	Company training	S.S.
11/1/16	"	S.S.
12/1/16	"	S.S.
13/1/16	"	S.S.
14/1/16	Brigade Exercise. Bat fell in 8.40 less A+B who formed advance guard under CAPT LEDWARD Bat took up a position facing S.E. from Lendwill to the BILLERICAY. Gt BURSTEAD RD. Boys training line in REAR.	S.S. Appendix A.
15/1/16	Bat close order drill under Adj.	S.S.
16/1/16	Church Parade 8.40 am. 2 offrs + 14 NCOs + men to BILLERICAY on Scout Service.	S.S.
17/1/16	22 men received from 3/4 Glrs. Company training	S.S.
18/1/16	13	Lecture Board on Officers	S.S.
19/1/16	Gymnasium Inspection	S.S.
20/1/16	Maj. Gen E T DICKSON Insp. Gen. of Inf. inspected the Bat whilst doing Company training	S.S.

(73989) W4141—463. 400,000. 9/14. H.&J.Ltd. Forms/C. 2118/10.

Army Form C. 2118.

WAR DIARY
or
INTELLIGENCE SUMMARY.
(Erase heading not required.)

Instructions regarding War Diaries and Intelligence Summaries are contained in F.S. Regs., Part II and the Staff Manual respectively. Title pages will be prepared in manuscript.

Hour, Date, Place		Summary of Events and Information	Remarks and references to Appendices
21.1.16	Breakwood	8 men received from 3/4 Glos. Company training.	ST.
22.1.16	"	Reg Exercise under Major Gwynn	ST.
23.1.16	"	Church parade 8.40 am.	ST.
24.1.16	"	100 short 111 rifles & bayonets received. Company training	ST.
25.1.16	"	G.O.C inspected Glos recruits at 11.30 am. Medical Board for all officers	ST. Appendix B.
26.1.16	"	Company training	ST.
27.1.16	"	Brigade Exercise. The Bat formed to left of an attack on an enemy in position between ST JOSEPHS & NW CHILDERDITCH SE end of THORNDON PARK. (Sheet 108)	ST. Appendix C.
28.1.16	"	LT. COL PIERCE went on leave. MAJOR SHELLARD took over command.	ST.
29.1.16	"	Bat close order drill under Bn Adj	ST.
30.1.16	"	Church parade 2 coys 8.40 am / at 10 am / at 10.45 am	ST.
31.1.16	"	Company training	ST.

Shellard. Major.
H/OC. 3/4 Glos Reg.

A.

2/4th Battalion Gloucester Regt.

Operation Orders. No. 37.   Copy No. 1

By Lt. Col. C. Pierce, Com'dg.   Brentwood. 13-1-16.

Ref ½ O.S. Sheet 30

	1. On the night of 13/14th Jan. 1916 - 61st Division billeted near BRENTWOOD - An invading force of all arms has landed at SOUTHEND and is moving on BILLERICAY with the apparent intention of cutting the LONDON main line of Railway.
2/1st R.F.A. Brigade. 183rd Infantry Brigade. 2/3rd S.M.F.Amb.	2. Troops as per margin Col Sir J. Barnsley commanding, will take up a defensive position S.E. of BILLERICAY at 11 a.m, delaying the enemy until the Division has taken up a defensive position along the main line of Railway.
Advance Guard. A & B Coys. 2/4th Glos. Regt. Commander Capt. Ledward. 2/4th Glos.Rgt.	3. The Advanced Guard composed as per margin will be ¾ mile ahead of Main body and will proceed from junction BRENTWOOD & INGATESTONE and INGRAVE RDS via HUTTON to point 323 S end of BILLERICAY.
	4. The Battalion (less A & B Coys) will be formed up in Westbury Road ready to march off at 8.45 a.m.
	5. The Brigade S.A.A.Res will be under the Command of Major Gwynn, 2/4th Bn. Gloster Regt.
	6. Cookers and Watercarts will be brigaded under an Officer to be notified later and will follow in rear of the 183rd Infantry Brigade S.A.A. Res.
Signallers.	7. The Officer i/c Signal Section will detail 2 cyclists to report to the O.C. Advance Guard at the starting point at 8.40 a.m, and 4 signallers.
	8. The C.O. will be at the head of the main body.
Scouts.	9. Report to Capt. Ledward, at Batt. Headquarters 8.15.a.m.

(signed) T.S. Foweraker,
Capt & Adjutant,
2/4th Gloucestershires.

Copy No. 1.   to Filed.
     2.   O.C. Advance Guard   by Orderly.
     3.   O.C. "C" Coy.   "
     4.   O.C. "D" "   "   at 12.30 p.m.
     5.   O i/c Transport   "   13. 1. 16.
     6.   O i/c Signal Sect.   "
     7.   O i/c Scouts.

B 9

Operation Orders No 10 –
By Lieut Col Pape
Comdg 2/4 Lond Regt

Ref 1" map sheet 108

1. A marauding force 1 Bn is known to be near MOUNTNESSING and intend raiding DODDINGHURST

2. The 2/4 Lond Regt is marching from BRENTWOOD via PILGRIMS HALL MILL FIELD DOGWOOD FARM. DODDINGHURST.

3. You will should the enemy be encountered reconnoitre the ground with a view to taking up a defensive position.

4. Head of column will pass junction SHENFIELD – ONGAR Rd at 9 a.m.

Operation Orders No 14
by Lt Col C Pierce
    OC 2/4 Glouc Regt   Brentwood.
  Ref 1" OS. sheet 108   26.1.16

An invading force of all arms reached EAST HORNDON on night Jan 26/27 and has taken up entrenched position at S end of THORNDON PARK.

2/1 RFA Bde
183rd Inf Bde   A force as per margin under Sir J BARNSLEY
2/3 (SM)FAmb will attack and destroy or capture enemy

Signal Sect   Starting point will be on LONDON-CHELMSFORD
(less 2 cyclists) road at X roads W of Bn BRENTWOOD.

A Coy   The Bn will parade in WESTBURY Rd
B   ready to march off at 9.30. in order as
C   per margin
D
Stretchers   Each man will carry 10 rds Blank
1st Line Trans ammunition (except recruits that have
port (less SAA not fired)
Bde Res Cookers
Water carts)   The O i/c Signallers will detail 2
                cyclists to report to the OC Advance
                gd at the starting point at 9.30 am

                Maj Guyim will command Bde SAA

Reserve and will issue orders to those concerned. They will follow in rear of the Batt^n which will pass starting point at 9.52 a.m.

The M.O will be in charge of the stretcher bearers and arrange for the conveyance of wounded to the Adv. Dressing station.

The O.C will be at the head of the Batt^n.

61 Division
183 Infantry Brigade
2/4 Batt. Gloucestershire Reg
Feb, Mar, April 1916 Missing

61st Division
183rd Brigade.

2/4th GLOUCESTER REGIMENT

23rd to 31st May 1916

Confidential.
2/4 Batt Gloster Rgt.

Army Form C. 2118.

WAR DIARY
or
INTELLIGENCE SUMMARY
(Erase heading not required.)

Instructions regarding War Diaries and Intelligence Summaries are contained in F. S. Regs., Part II. and the Staff Manual respectively. Title Pages will be prepared in manuscript.

Place	Date	Hour	Summary of Events and Information	Remarks and references to Appendices
TIDWORTH	23-5-16	9.15	Battalion moved to Southampton by two trains	
"		9.15	First train left TIDWORTH Personnel 20 officers 450 other ranks 1 first line transport	
"		10.25	Second train left " " 15 officers 438 " " remainder of "	
SOUTHAMPTON		11.45	First train arrived at Southampton SOUTHAMPTON	
"		12.48	Second " " " " "	
"		6.45	29 Officers + 746 O.R.s embarked on S.S. MARGUERITE. Transport completed. 6 officers 115 O.R.s entrained on S.S. BELEROPHON	
	24-5-16	12.35	Ships turned around + headed for SOUTHAMPTON	
SOUTHAMPTON		4 am	Reached SOUTHAMPTON	
"		7 pm	Ships sailed. Personnel of S.S. MARGUERITE disembarked. noted in sheds area all day	
		6 pm	Battalion again embarked on same ships Personnel became also 1 officer Lt C M PRITCHARD	
HAVRE	25-5-16	3.15 am	Ships arrived at HAVRE	
		8 am	Battalion disembarked & marched to DOCKS REST CAMP No 5	
	26-5-16	5 am	25 officers & 635 other ranks entrain at HAVRE (move to BERGETTE Transport arrived also moved in this Train.)	
		12 nn	6 officers 2.50 O.R.s entrain at HAVRE Route of Rail: HAVRE - ROVEN - A'BIN COURT -	App 1
			BOULOGNE - BERGETTE.	
	27-5-16	4.00 am	First Train arrived at BERGETTE (JE of AIRE) O15 d 66.36.A	
		4 pm	Second Train arrived at " P 19 36.A Marched to Billets	
		7 pm	Marched to LA PIERRIÈRE	
		—	Company Training	
	28-6-16	—	" "	
	29-5-16	—	" "	
	30-5-16	—	" "	
	31-5-16	12.30	Recd orders from 183rd Bde to furnish training in Trench work at LES LOBES. (FESTUBERT Sec) R.32 c.d.36+ M	add 2
		6.30 am	Batt moved with 183rd BDE to training area LELOBES where Batt came under orders of 106th Inf Bde 35 Div'n	add 2
		12.15	Arrived at LE LOBES Batt put into billets (2) this station awaited to proceed to Section allotted in the	add 3
		2	line for Batt training orders for move recd	add 4
			Casualties from 23-5-16 to 31-5-16	M

J.A. Tupman
LtCol.

1/20,000

2/4 Glosters

La Pierrière

Ref. Sheet 36A
O & P

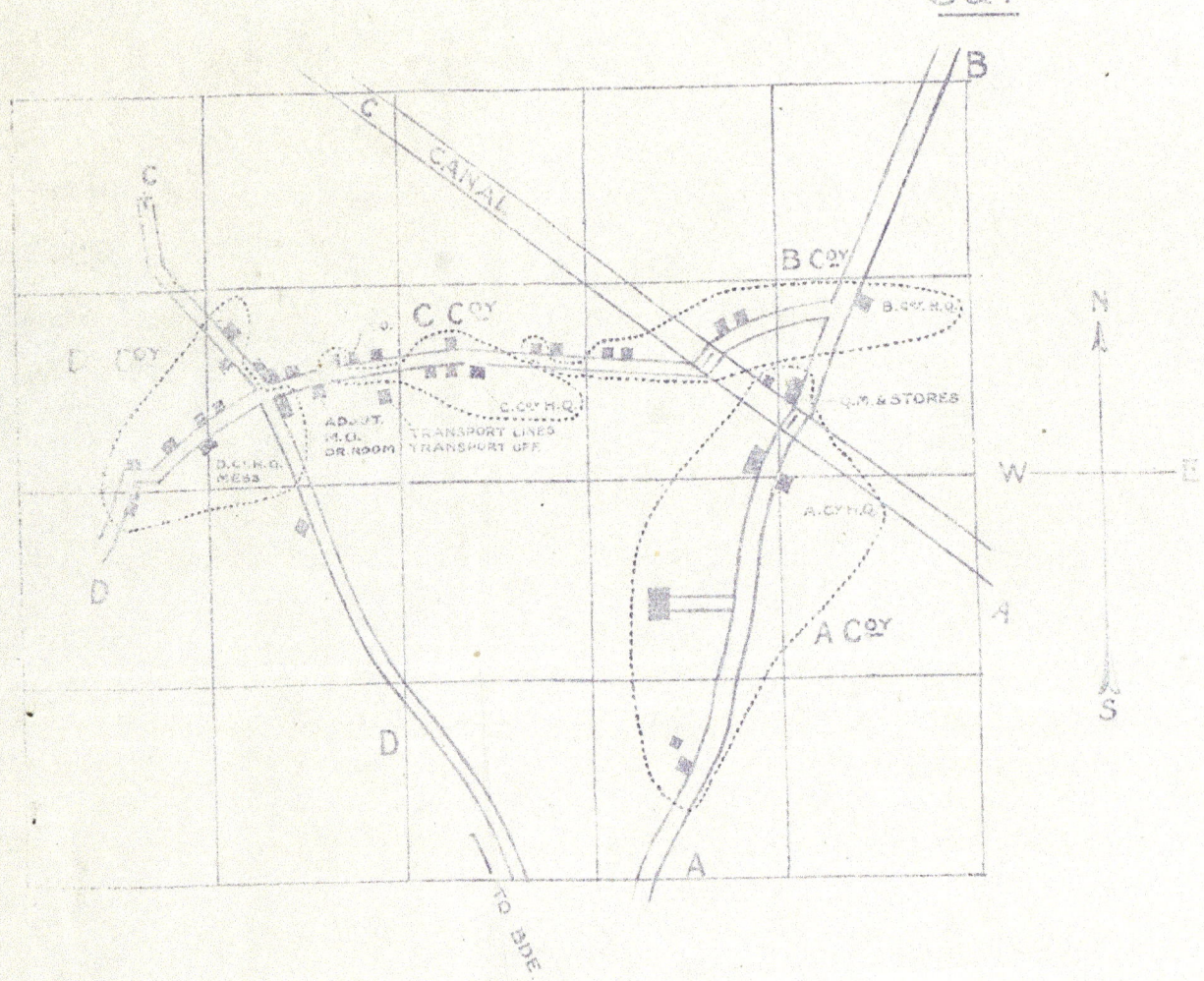

SECRET.   2/4th Bn. Gloster Regt.   Appendix 2

                           Battalion Orders.

By Lt. Col J.A.Tupman. Com'dg.   In the field.

Ref Map 36a.

1
Intention.   The Battalion will move from present station 31-5-16.

2
Order of march   See appendix attached.
& starting pt.

3
Rations.   Supplies for the 31st inst. will be carried on the Cookers
                      and on the man. Rations for June 1st will be carried
                      in Supply waggons.

4
Billets.   Greatest care is to be taken to leave all billets clean &
                      tidy. All paper, maps of billeting area and any document
                      of no further use should be burnt.

5
Latrines.   All latrines must be filled in and marked in stones by with
                      letter "L"

6
Breakfast.   Breakfast in Companies and Details will not be later than
                      5.15 am.

7.
Baggage.   Baggage will be dumped as under, to be collected by the
                      Transport:-
                            Headquarters & "C" and "D" Coys   -   Headqtrs Yard.
                            Q.M.Stores and "A" and "B" Coys   -   Q.M.Stores.
                      All baggage must be ready for loading at 5.15 am

8
Watches.   Signallers watches in Companies will be sent to Headquarters
                      to be synchronised at 8 pm this evening.

9
Baggage Guard.   Q.M. will find baggage guard for Transport.

10
Transport.   Transport will proceed on a different route to Starting Pt.
                      see appendix.

Reports   *at head of Column after 6.30 Office closed at 6 am*

                                        (Signed) T.S.Foworaker,
                                                  Capt & Adjt
                                                  2/4th Gloucestershires.

        No.1 - Filed.
        No.2 - Headquarters.
        No.3 - O.C. A Coy.
        No.4 - O.C. B Coy.
        No.5 - O.C. C Coy.
        No.6 - O.C. D Coy.
        No.7 - Detail Sections.

APPENDIX.

Order of March.	Starting Point.	Time of passing Starting Pt.	Route.	Remarks.
Signalling Sect & Headquarters.	T.30b 1.3.	6.30 am.	Nearest way to Starting Pt.	
"A" Coy.	-do-	6.31 am	-do-	
"B" "	-do-	6.32 am	-do-	
"C" "	-do-	6.33 am	-do-	
"D" "	-do-	6.34 am	-do-	
Machine Gun Section.	-do-	6.35 am	-do-	
Transport.	------	------	Transport field P.19a 3.3. P.26c 1.5. KKKK P.27a 10.8.	Transport will follow in rear of column on reaching point P.27a 10.8. Transport will arrange to reach this point at 6.40 am.

SECRET.   2/4th Bn. Gloster Regt.
                               Battalion Orders.   Appendix 3
By Lt. Col J.A.Tupman. Com'dg.   In the field.

Ref Map 56a.

1 Intention. The Battalion will move from present station 31-5-16.

2 Order of march & starting pt. See appendix attached.

3 Rations. Supplies for the 31st inst. will be carried on the Cookers and on the man. Rations for June 1st will be carried in Supply waggons.

4 Billets. Greatest care is to be taken to leave all billets clean & tidy. All paper, maps of billeting area and any documents of no further use should be burnt.

5 Latrines. All latrines must be filled in and marked in stones with letter "L"

6 Breakfast. Breakfast in Companies and Details will not be later than 5.15 am.

7. Baggage. Baggage will be dumped as under, to be collected by the Transport:-
   Headquarters & "C" and "D" Coys   -   Headqtrs Yard.
   Q.M.Stores and "A" and "B" Coys   -   Q.M.Stores.
All baggage must be ready for loading at 5.15 am

8 Watches. Signallers watches in Companies will be sent to Headquarters to be synchronised at 8 pm this evening.

9 Baggage Guard. Q.M. will find baggage guard for Transport.

10 Transport. Transport will proceed on a different route to Starting Pt. see appendix.

Reports. *at head of column after 6.30 Office closes at 6. am*

                                    (Signed) T.S.Foweraker,
                                             Capt & Adjt
                                             2/4th Gloucestershires.

   No.1 - Filed.
   No.2 - Headquarters.
   No.3 - O.C. A Coy.
   No.4 - O.C. B Coy.
   No.5 - O.C. C Coy.
   No.6 - O.C. D Coy.
   No.7 - Detail Sections.

Athlone 4

Casualties since leaving Sidworth.

2/Lt Pritchard CH. returned sick from Southampton.
3/Lt McHutchings } Admitted Hants Hospital 25.5.16
Capt - Roach }
5112 - Mees
12291 - Baker   Missing — en route from France. now no trace[?]
3633 - Livings   Missing en route from France — rejoined 27-5-16
3139 - Briggs }
15211 - Griffen Missing en route from France — rejoined 28.5.16 — admitted to
                 2/3rd S.M.F. Hosp. 29-5-16.
Lt Litchand   } transferred to A.P.M. 30/5/16.
Lt Sandell   }
— bor   }
             4   Admitted to Hosp.   3/5/16.
             5   Bryd. Orderling party at 1st Mor. Hosp. 31/5/16
             2   Seventeen bouqht
             3   Africas sick

Confidential.
War Diary
of
29th Bn Gloucestershire Regiment
from June 1st 1916 to June 30th 1916.

(Volume 1).

WAR DIARY or INTELLIGENCE SUMMARY

Army Form C. 2118.

2/4 Batt Gloster Regiment

Place	Date	Hour	Summary of Events and Information	Remarks and references to Appendices
LES LOBES	June 1st	10 am	Arrived BETHUNE (combined Rly) 36A SE 36 SW 36B NE 36 C NW. C & D Coys move to 10th Battalions for instruction in trench warfare. C to LE TOURET X.16.d.2.9 (1/9 Durh L.I.) D to Rue HAMEL X.20.d.4.5 (1/5 H.L.I.) Made Quarters A Coy + B Coy move to 11 wks battalions for instruction. H.26.d.+ A Coy to X.11.a.9.9 (1/4 Royal Scots) B Coy X.21.a.9.9/14" Yorks W — Training 6 days in line 4 days Batt during "10 6" Trenches in Trenches A + 6 Officers — 173 OR's B 6 Officers — 147 OR's C 6 Officers — 190 OR's D 4 Officers — 171 OR's	
	2nd		Coys attached as above for instruction	
	3rd		"	
	4th		"	
	5th		A Coys changes position with D Coy. B Coy changes with C Coy. A2 Cheshires Batt. B2 A2 + 24	
	6/7/8		Instruction Coys attached as above	
	9th	10 pm	Batt completes instruction. Marches to LES LOBES R.32.C. billets for the night	
LES LOBES	10th	—	Batt rests for the day. Orders for move to RIEZ BAILLEUL received from Bde	See Appendix I
		9 pm	orders for move to RIEZ BAILLEUL issued to coys	
RIEZ BAILLEUL	11th	10 am	Batt arrives to RIEZ BAILLEUL M.7.d from 10 LILLE	
		4 hr	1 Platoon (D) sent to ROUGE CROIX M.27.A.n.8. to take over posts	
		11 hr	1 Platoon (D) sent to LUDHIANA POST to take over post from 1/5" ROYAL WELSH REG M.34 + 36	
	12th		Company Training	
	13th		"	

Ref: BETHUNE (contd from ?) Army Form C. 2118.
2/4 Glosters Regt.

WAR DIARY
or
INTELLIGENCE SUMMARY.
(Erase heading not required.)

Instructions regarding War Diaries and Intelligence Summaries are contained in F. S. Regs., Part II. and the Staff Manual respectively. Title pages will be prepared in manuscript.

Place	Date	Hour	Summary of Events and Information	Remarks and references to Appendices
RIEZ BAILLEUL M.7	June 15th	—	Company Training. Battalion bathed at PONT REMUEL	
		3.30	Bath taken over by units in MOATED GRANGE Road (right sub sec) from 2/8 WORCESTER	
		9.30	Relief Section of D Coy Taken over by B Coy and located at M.35 d.5.5	
	16th	12.15	Coys taken over. Staff H.Q established at M.35 d.5.5	
			Relief complete. A Coy major B Coy centre C Coy right. D Coy in support. Support House	
A 29 a 6.3 M.7 21 a 8.3	17th	2.35	L6-FINNIES TAPPY STREET & TILLELOY at Garrisoned by D Coy	
			Gas alarm after trench mortar attack was reported between about 2a.m 15 Germans were	
A 29 a 6.3 M.35 d 6.5	18th	12.40	Fired my men antillery, at Germans front but retreated M.29l enemy front line of M.36 c	
Dwe lower dugouts from M.35 a 2 a5 M.29 a no 5		5.30am	Some damage inflicted on M.35 c.5.5	
	19th	12.15am	Our artillery opened fire on enterprised attacks M.35 2 M.35 3 enemy looked for 3 hours the enemy retaliated slightly	
		9.10am	Enemy with their trench mortars line on 5.1915 M.30 c.2.19 Lining lasted 1 hour	
		10.30pm	Our artillery bombarded enemys trenches from M.36 c.3.6 to M.36A 5.7 keeping lasting 20 mins	
	20	1.30am	Enemy opened fire and bombed on M.36 a.1.2 Relief of M35c by M.36 No 3535 Pte Hyland	See Appx
	21	11.25	M.29 d.2.0 R.E. Pte died from Bayliss, wound received north trench alarm sounded for duration	
			Relieved by 2/6 Battn moved Hd. Batt return to billet at RIEZ BAILLEUL M 7 a.0.	
RIEZ BAILLEUL M.7 a	22	—	Batt training in W.H.G area (Divisional Reserve)	
	23 to 30	—	" " " " "	Orders to proceed Nursile, France.

J. G. Turner Lt Col

2/4th Bn. Gloster Regt.   SECRET.

Operation Orders. No. 6.

By Lt. Col. J.A.Tupman. Com'dg.   In the Field. 10-6-16
Ref. Combined Map. Bethune.

1. Intention. 2/4th Bn. Gloster Regt will relieve the 15th Bn. Royal Welsh Fus: at RIEZ BAILLEUL at 12 noon to-morrow 11th inst.

2. Route. See appendix attached.

3. Starting Point. See appendix attached.

4. Posts. O.C. "D" Coy will detail half a platoon for posts at M.27.B.1.8. and half a platoon for post at M 27.B.4.4. These parties to proceed to positions mentioned on reaching REIZ BAILLEUL.

5. Transport. Transport will move in rear of Battalion, as laid down in Divisional Standing Orders, page 22.
G.S.Waggons will be in the rear.
O.C. "A" Coy will furnish a baggage guard to march with Transport of 1 N.C.O. and 6 men.
The Transport Officer will arrange for a limber to call at Company Headquarters at the following times :-
"A" Coy.   8.30 am.   "B" Coy   9.15 am
"D" "   8.45 am   "C" "   9.30 am.

6. Billets. All Billets at LES LOBES are to be left clean.
O.C. Coys will render a certificate to the C.O. that this order has been complied with.
No men must be left in billets to clean up.

7. Lewis Guns. Lewis Guns of Battalions in supports will be in front line. Lewis Guns of the 2/4th Glosters will be attached, and under orders of the Officer Commanding 2/8th Worcester Regt.. The Section must be ready to proceed where they may be wanted.

8. Trench Stores. O.C. Coys will check carefully all Trench stores taken over. Receipts will be sent to Battalion Headquarters as soon as possible.

9. Movements. All movements of troops East of the BELLE CROIX - LA BASSE ROAD will be by Platoon, 100yds interval by day and 50 yds interval by night.
Vehicles will move by threes, the same interval.

10. Baggage. All Company and Officers Baggage must be brought to the Quartermaster's stores by Transport waggon which will call at Company Headquarters at times stated above.

11. Orderlies. Coys will detail one orderly to report at Batt.Hdqrs as soon as possible after arrival.

(Signed)   T.S.Foweraker,
           Capt & Adjt,
           2/4th. Gloucestershires.

No 1 Copy - War Diary.
   2 "   - Retained.
   3 "   - O.C. "A" Coy.
   4 "   - O.C. "B" "
   5 "   - O.C. "C" "
   6 "   - O.C. "D" "
   7 "   - Transport Officer.

2/rth Bn. Gloster Regt.

APPENDIX.

Coy.	Route.	Starting Pt.	Time passing Starting Pt.
Headquarters & "A" Coy.	LES LOBES ZELOBES x roads at FOSSE (R 21.1.4.) LE MARAIS FME. REZ BAILLEUL	R.32 B.4.2.	10. 0.am
"B" Coy	-do-	-do-	10.1.am
"C" "	-do-	-do-	10.2.am
"D" "	-do-	-do-	10.3.am
Lewis Gun Sct.) Transport.)	-do-	-do-	10.4.am.

(Signed) T.S.Fowersker,
Capt &Adjt,
2/4th Gloucestershires.

2/4th Battalion Gloucestershire Regiment. Appendix 2

BATTALION ORDERS, No.15.   Copy No. 2

By Lieut. Col. J. A. Tupman, Comdg.   In the field, 20-6-16.

Ref. 1/40,000 sheet 36.A.

1. Intention. The 2/4th Glosters will be relieved on the 21st inst. and night of 21st/22nd insts. and will return to billets at REIZ BAILLEUL.

2. Details. Signallers, Snipers & Lewis Gunners will be relieved in the afternoon.

3. Companies. Companies will be relieved at night.

4. Guides. Sniping Officer & Guides, Bombing Officer (2/Lt.Thacker) Signalling Officer & Guides, Lewis Gun Officer & Guides, & 1 Guide per company, will be at police post SOUTH TILLELOY STREET at 3 p.m. to meet Details mentioned in Trench Standing Order 10 .B.
Guides for Reserve Company will be at ROUGE CROIX at 4 p.m.
" Left " (Fire line) " 9 "
" Right " " " 9.30 p.m.
" Centre " " " 10 "

5. Communication Trenches. No parties of companies of 2/4th Glos. will move down communication trenches until all relieving battalion is in position in trenches.

6. Trench Stores. All Battalion trench stores, i.e. periscopes, very pistols, grenade rifles (if any) and all stores on charge of battalion will be taken to billets by coys. Trench stores belonging to sector will be handed over to relieving battalion. O.C. Coys. will prepare lists of these before relief in duplicate; one receipt will be sent to Batt. H.Q. (Adjutant); the duplicate will be handed to relieving troops.

7. Trenches. O.C. Coys. will be responsible that all trenches are absolutely clean and tidy on handing over. All rubbish & tins will be buried not burnt. Latrines must receive special attention.

8. Completion of relief. O.C. Coys. will inform Batt. H.Q. <u>immediately</u> relief is complete by code word.

9. Movements. Companies will move independently to billets.
All movements of troops along or east of the BELLE CROIX - LA BASSEE ROAD will be by platoons at 100 yards distance by day and 50 yards distance at night.
Wagons & carts will move by threes at same distance.

(Signed) T. S. Foweraker,
Capt. &Adjut.,
2/4th Glos.

Issued at 6.45 p.m. 20-6-16.

Copy No. 1   183 Inf. Bde.
2   War Diary.
3   C.O.
4   O.C. A. Coy.
5   "   B   "
6   "   C   "
7   "   D   "
8   Lewis Gun Officer.
9   Sniping Officer.
10 Signalling Officer.
11 2/5th Warwicks.

2/4th Battalion Gloucestershire Regiment.

Casualties for month ending June 30th 1916.

3927 Pte.	Vance.	Killed in action 6-6-16.	
5062 "	Tyler.	Wounded in action 7-6-16.	
5125 "	Gaines.	Killed in action 8-6-16.	
3122 "	Russell H.	Wounded in action 4-6-16.	
4452 "	Hill H.	Wounded in action 1-6-16.	
4420 "	Aplin.	Killed in action 16-6-16.	
5063 Cpl.	Fleming W.	Wounded in action 17-6-16.	
5062 Pte.	Scott.	Wounded in action 20-6-16.	D. of W. 20-6-16.
2048 "	Davis.	Wounded in action 20-6-16.	
1750 "	Callas.	Wounded in action 19-6-16.	Ret'd to duty.
5208 "	Fellinor.	Wounded in action 19-6-16.	do.
1813 "	Dodkin.	Wounded in action 19-6-16.	D. of W. 22-6-16.
1544 "	Lake.	Wounded in action 20-6-16.	Ret'd 26-6-16.
2564 "	Foster.	Wounded in action 21-6-16.	
3288 L/S.	Wilcox C.A.	Wounded in action 21-6-16.	
3855 Pte.	Davey.	Wounded in action 21-6-16.	
1445 "	Carver.	Shell Shock 21-6-16.	
2495 Drm.	Luke E.	Wounded in action 21-6-16.	Ret'd 24-6-16.
3346 Pte.	Little.	Accidentally wounded 24-6-16.	
3356 Sgt.	Brinicombe E.	Accidentally wounded 29-6-16.	
3 687 Cpl.	Taylor E.A.	do.	
2947 Pte.	George S.	do.	
4426 "	Cousins.	do.	Ret'd to duty.
2319 "	Fancy.	do.	do.
2nd Lieut.	E.L. Moore.	do.	
Lieut.	R.M. Hadingham.	Missing.	

Vol III

CONFIDENTIAL.

War Diary of
2/4th Battalion, Gloucestershire Regt

from 1st July 1916 to 31st July 1916.

Volume 3

Army Form C. 2118.

2/4th Batt. Gloucestershire Regt.

WAR DIARY
INTELLIGENCE SUMMARY
(Erase heading not required.)

Instructions regarding War Diaries and Intelligence Summaries are contained in F.S. Regs., Part II. and the Staff Manual respectively. Title Pages will be prepared in manuscript.

Place	Date	Hour	Summary of Events and Information	Remarks and references to Appendices
RIEZ BAILLEUL	1.7.16		Battalion Training. Casualties: Accdt. Killed - 1 O/R. Accdt Wounded - Lt. F.L. HALL & 1 O/R.	
"	2.7.16		Battalion Training. Casualties: Accdt Killed - 1 O/R. Accdt. Wounded. 2 O/R.	
"	3.7.16		Battalion Training. Two A.A. shells fell just outside Battn. HQ. One was a Dud; the other burst and slightly wounded the Adjutant. (Capt. Forrester) in the arm and the orderly over HQrs, in the leg. Further Casualties - Wounded. 1 O/R.	
FRONT - FAUQUISSART SUB. SECN.	"	10.30pm	Relief of Trenches complete. Line taken over from 2/4 Oxf & Bucks L.I. Casualties -	Appx. A.
" night	{4.7.16 / 5.7.16}		Raid on Enemy's trenches by 'C' Coy. See Report by Lt. Col. Commanding. Casualties: {Killed Capt. F.J. HANNAM & 6 O/R. Wounded - 2Lt E.O. JAGO, Lt. O.A. WILLIAMSON, & 48 O/R. Accdt. Wounded. 1 O/R. Missing - 7 O/R.} rest to duty	
"	5.7.16		Day Quiet. Both sides repairing damage of the Artillery Fire. Enemy fired HE & shrapnel in our forward C.T.s. Our men wounded in Abbey lines. Casualties -	
"		10pm - 11 am		
"	6.7.16		Congratulations received from Corps Commander on 'C' Coy's having entered German lines on night of 4th/5th July.	
"		5 pm	Artillery Front adjusted to follows:- D Coy. Bays 1-35, B Coy. Bays 36-70, C Coy. Bays 71-90, and A Coy. Bays 91-106. Casualties - Killed 2 O/R. Wounded - 11 O/R.	
"	7.7.16		Apparent Change in Enemy Opposite us. Sniping much more active - M.G. fire less. Casualties - Wounded - 1 O/R.	
"	8.7.16		Day Quiet.	
"		10pm - 10.30pm	Enemy Artillery Fire more Vigorous than usual. Casualties - Wounded 2 O/R. Accdt Wounded 1 O/R.	

Army Form C. 2118.

WAR DIARY (2)
INTELLIGENCE SUMMARY

2/4 Batt. Gloucestershire Regt.

(Erase heading not required.)

Instructions regarding War Diaries and Intelligence Summaries are contained in F. S. Regs., Part II. and the Staff Manual respectively. Title Pages will be prepared in manuscript.

Place	Date	Hour	Summary of Events and Information	Remarks and references to Appendices
FROQUISSART SUB. SECN.	9-7-16	5-30pm	Battalion was relieved during day by 2/6th Gloucesters. Relief Complete. Battalion became Bde. Res. Battn.	
LAVENTIE	"		A & C Coys in Billets. B & D Coys in POL2 Behind Reserve Lines. Casualties :- Wounded 3 O/R. Capt. D.G. BARNSLEY (2/4 Gloster seconded for duty as Adjt. 48 Base Depot. HAVRE) rejoined Battalion for duty. Appointed Acting Adjutant, vice Capt. T.S. FOWERAKER, Wounded.	See entry under date 3-7-16
"	10-7-16	6am - 8-15am	Enemy Artillery active. Several Incendiary Shells fell near Billets. Company Training. Fatigues.	
"	11-7-16		Company Training. Fatigues. Bathing for HQ details & C Coy. Casualties - Wounded 1 O/R	
"	12-7-16	8am -10am	Bathing for half each B & D Coys. Company Training & Fatigues.	
"	13-7-16	8am -11am	Bathing for remaining half each B & D Coys. Company Training & Fatigues. Further message received from Corps Commander reading Congratulations on arrival of raids night 4th/5th July - this having been the most successful Minor raid so far - believed. Casualties - 1 O/R	
"	14-7-16		Company Training.	
FROQUISSART SUB-SECN.	15-7-16	6.30am 5am	Relief orders received. Relief complete. Our front :- SUTHERLAND AV - BURLINGTON ARCADE taken over from 2/6 Glosters. A Coy. left Coy. D Coy. Right Coy. B Coy at DEAD END POST. C Coy at LAVENTIE EAST and HOUFOMONT. Casualties :- Wounded 1 O/R (not 15 July) accdt wound. 1 O/R	

2449 Wt. W14957/M90 759,000 1/16 J.B.C. & A. Forms/C.2118/12.

WAR DIARY
INTELLIGENCE SUMMARY

2/4th Batt. Gloucestershire Regt.

Army Form C. 2118.

Place	Date	Hour	Summary of Events and Information	Remarks and references to Appendices
FAUQUISSART SUR-SECM	16.7.16	7.30 am	Hqrs moved to Battle Hqrs. (N.7.c.1.9. Map 10000) Casualties :- Wounded 20 O/R. Killed 1 O/R. Accdt. Wounded 2 O/R.	
"	17.7.16		Little activity on either side. A & D Coys to Billets LEVANTIE. B + C (less 2 platoons) in Front Line. 2 platoons C. in Reserve. Casualties :- Wounded 9 O/R.	
"	18.7.16		A & D Coys to Front Line. B in Support. C in Reserve. Casualties - Killed 2 O/R. Wounded 7 O/R.	
"	19.7.16	11 am 6 pm	Bombardment of Enemy Trenches Commenced. Assault launched. See Report on Action by Lt Col Commander. Casualties:- Killed. Lt R.G.SCRASE, 2/Lt D.C. JAMES + 18 O/R. Wounded. (Capt E.H.E. WOODWARD, Lt. A.H. DIXON, 2/Lt. H.P. KAUFMANN, 2/Lt. H.F.M. PELLATT, + 2/Lt E.O. JAGO. + 118 O/R. Missing - 19 O/R.	Appendix B (X)
"	20.7.16	2am 7-15am 4.15pm 8pm	Relief by 2/7 Worcester Regt. (B4) All our wounded cleared from Trenches. Battalion moved to LEVANTIE. Battalion moved to ESTAIRES. Lt.Col. TUPMAN to Hospital, MERVILLE. Command of Battalion taken over by Major R.E. BOULTON. (Second in Command) (B4) Battalion complete. Casualties :- nil	
ESTAIRES	21.7.16		Company Training; Kit and Clothing Inspection - deficiencies made up. Casualties :- nil	

WAR DIARY
(4) 1/4th Batt. Gloucester Reg.t
INTELLIGENCE SUMMARY

Army Form C. 2118.

(Erase heading not required.)

Place	Date	Hour	Summary of Events and Information	Remarks and references to Appendices
ESTAIRES	22.7.16	11.30am	Battalion Inspection by G.O.C. Division.	
		4.30pm – 6.45pm	Bathing. A, B, C & D Coys. Hqrs. & Transport.	
	23.7.16	10am	Church Parade.	
LEVANTIE	24.7.16	8.15am	Battalion moved to LEVANTIE. A, B & D Coys.} in Billets. C Coy. in Bullet – HOSPOMONT. (See 1 Plat-5)	1st Army Orders to XI Corps MS 964 25/7/16 MS GHQ 7.9.16
			DEAD END & PICANTIN. Company Training. Fatigues.	
	25.7.16		Company Training. Fatigues. Appointment of Major R.E. BOULTON, K.O.Y.L.I., to Temporary Command of 1/4 Glost. R. approved.	
FAUQUISSART SUB-SECN	26.7.16	5am 9.30am	Relief of 1/7 Warwicks commenced. Trenches :– BOND ST – ROTTEN ROW Relief complete. Disposition in Trenches :– A Coy. Bays 102–117, D Coy. Bays 66–101, C Coy. Bays 35–65, and B Coy. Bays 1–34. 2/Lt G.A. EDWARDS & 11 O.R. left for Course of Sniping School. Casualties :– nil	
"	27.7.16		Artillery active during morning. 'A' Coy. 1/6 Gloster Placed temporarily disposal of the 1/4 Glosters to recover (in Poste HOSPOMONT. DEAD END & PICANTIN.) 2/Lt F.A. RIDLER presented with Military Cross at MERVILLE, for gallantry during night 4/5/7/16 1916 (LaBrelle) :– Wounded 1 O/R	

Army Form C. 2118.

WAR DIARY
(5) 1/4 Batt Gloster Regt.
or
INTELLIGENCE SUMMARY
(Erase heading not required.)

Instructions regarding War Diaries and Intelligence Summaries are contained in F. S. Regs., Part II. and the Staff Manual respectively. Title Pages will be prepared in manuscript.

Place	Date	Hour	Summary of Events and Information	Remarks and references to Appendices
ANGOULEME SUB-SECN	28.7.16		Artillerie and aircraft activity on both sides. Casualties :- nil.	
"	29.7.16	10.25 pm to 11.15 pm	Our Left Group R.A. fired on SUGAR LOAF. We replied with rifle grenade fire. Casualties :- Killed. Capt. J.S. FOOT of 1/4R.	
"	30.7.16		Quiet day. Lt. A.E. OWEN and 7 NCOs left for Physical Training & Bayonet Fighting Course. Casualties :- nil.	
"	31.7.16	10.20 am	Orders for Relief received. Casualties :- Wounded 1 O/R.	
			(X) Alfred B— has been forwarded to Base Office at Tufanan (in England, Sick.) Mrs Alyn in his possession. Then will be forwarded later.	

R.B. Boulton Major
Commanding 1/4 Gloucesters.

LEVANTE
1. VIII. 16

183 BRIGADE.

I have to report with reference to the raid carried out by my Battn. last night that the Company under the command of Capt. F.J.Hanham left our trenches at 12.40 a.m. and gained the enemy's parapet at 1.20 a.m. without drawing fire to any extent only two men being wounded by bullets on the way over. Captain Hanham led the bombing parties into the enemys parapet through the wire which was well cut, with the greatest gallantry in the face of bombs and Machine Gun fire which was opened as our parties reached the wire. Captain Hanham cleared one bay with his revolver and a fierce bomb fight occured which I could see from where I was and during which, all there agree, 15 to 20 Germans were killed.

At about 1.30 Captain Hanham was hit in the leg with a bullet and had to be carried out by Pte May and Pte Allen.

Lieut. F.A.Ridler who had gained the parapet by this time then assumed command and at 1.35 a.m. found it impossible to maintain his hold on the trench, Sgt Hyde and Pte.Godwin Cox and Franklin who had also gained the trench being either killed or taken prisoner.

The following also gained the trench, Pte Pearce and Pte Millard and escaped unwounded, L/Cpl.Hill and Pte Everett also got into the trench but were wounded.
Lt.Ridler also reports the excellent work done by Pte Hudd who was seen to bayonet a German and take on three more single handed, he escaped unwounded but was wounded on the way back.

The other two platoon Officers 2/Lt.E.O.Jago and 2/Lt. O.A.Williamson were outside the wire endeavouring to keep the men together and encouraging them in every way possible. Severe casualties occured on the way back. Lt Ridler and Pte Allen and Pte Tone did not return to our lines till about 3 and until all wounded men had been brought in.

The 4 Company Stretcher bearers did excellent work in assisting with the wounded in "NO MAN's LAND" of those Pte Nash did particular good work in bringing in the wounded.

Pte Newbery also behaved with great coolness on the German parapet with Lt.Ridler and brought in two wounded men himself.

Pte Martin also assisted Lt.Ridler to bring in one wounded man as did Pte Coulston.

The Company Sergeant Major Peart who was with Captain Hanham carried a wounded man on his back for about 30 yards when the man on his back was killed. Sgt.Major Peart was afterwards hit in the heal. This raid was performed after a heavy bombardment or our trenches by the Germans.

I desire to recommend Captain Frederick J.Hanham who died from his wound soon after reaching our trenches for the Victoria Cross as it was undoubtedly due to his splendid dash and courage and noble example that our party reached the enemy's parapet.

I wish to recommend 2/Lieut.Frederick Arnold Ridler 2/4 Glosters for the Military Cross for his ably seconding his Company Commander and his loyalty and devotion to his men in remaining out until all the wounded had been brought in. He showed a splendid example of what an Officer should be.

I also desire to recommend the following for a Military award.

Cont.

2568 Compy. Sgt.Major William S.Peart 2/4 Glosters

4643	Pte	Jack Hudd	do.
3324	"	Henry May	do.
3885	Drummer	Edward Newberry	do.
3377	A/Lce.Cpl.	Arthur Hill	do.
6251	Pte.	Leonard Everett	do.
6248	Pte.	Harold Allen.	do.
4359	Pte.	William James True	do.
5165	Pte.	John James Nash	do.

The strength of raiding party was 4 Officers 132 O.R. not including an R.E. party of 2 N.C.O's and 4 men.

5.7.16.
(Sgd) J.A.Tupman Lt Col.
O.C.2/4th Glosters.

The casualties in raid were :-

Captain Frank J.Hanham Wounded (died of wounds)

2/Lt.O Allison Williamson Wounded.

Other Ranks.   Killed 2.   Wounded 28.

Missing 8.   Shock 1.

The O.C. C. Coy.

for an hour.

You will attack and hold, the portion of
the enemy's trenches marked on the attached
map.

Dummies ✓   Whistles.
Boots nailed   Rose care-
Coats off.   Pans horned.
German Hands up
Come on

                                               o Bombing By
           B.P.?   to F.L.
activity: ~~F.L.~~ Wire cutters
           2. Bombing Parties around the dug saps to F.L.
                                                        S.L.
                to
           Reserves Platoon for support line.
                              Front Line.

                                              4/5 July 1916?

B   COPY.   FOR ATTACHMENT TO WAR DIARY
183rd Inf. Bde.   2/4th GLOUCESTER REGT
                             for month of JULY 1916

With reference to the operations of the 19th inst. I have to make the following report.

At 5.31 pm. the time ordered for deployment in NO MANS LAND, A.Coy. (the left assault) filed out through Sap 7a and successfully deployed 3 platoons in accordance with my orders.

D.Coy. (the Right assault) was delayed for a few minutes, and by 5.50 pm. had its leading platoon well deployed in NO MANS LAND, the next platoon of this forming the 2nd wave were partly out. At this point in the operations a heavy machine gun fire was opened on D.Coy. in the open, and the men were driven back on me into the Sally Port of sap 9 where I was standing. This Machine gun fire was particularly heavy and appeared to come from the Front, and Right Front from at least 5 or 6 M.Gs.

At 5.55 pm. I received a report saying A.Coy. was pushing on all right and I at once ordered the 2nd, 3rd, & 4th waves of D.Coy. to be moved to the other Sally Port (No.7a), and gave the Officers orders to push out there as rapidly as possible and to work up to the Right of A.Coy. I then went to the Sally Port (7a) and on arriving there found that A.Coy. by that time 6.10 pm. had also been driven back. I then ordered that the men should be collected and all to be ready for a push forward should the opportunity occur. At the time I considered further attempt to advance in the face of this M.G. fire useless.

I communicated with the 6th Glosters on my Right, these events as they occurred.

At 6.15 pm. I received information that the attack on my left had also failed, but I was unable to ascertain the state of affairs on my right.

At 8.0 pm. I received an order to attack again at 9.0 pm., with the Companies not previously engaged - this was done, but only 1 Lewis Gun could be found available, 3 being out in NO MANS LAND; of the other 3, 1 was in the reserve trench (under orders to come up), 1 was ready, and the 3rd was hung up to the Right Sally Port. These guns have all been recovered with the exception of 1 left in the trench last night, and which has been sent for.

The behaviour of both Officers and men, under very trying circumstances was excellent and I very much regret A., & D.Coy. did not get an opportunity of proving their mettle, as they went forward for the assault in a most gallant manner. The conduct of their Officers, Captain E.H.E.Woodward (wounded) and Lieutenants R.G.Scrase and J.C.James (both killed) in particular, being beyond praise.

After we had been driven back, there were many instances of men going out to assist to bring in the wounded. When it got dark I also sent out 2 patrols.

Of the 30 Trained Lewis Gunners there are only 20 left. The 13 Lewis Gunners who went out with the 2 guns of A.Coy. were reduced to three, and I desire to bring to your notice the devotion to duty shewn by L/Cpl. Porter, and Privates Burge and Denning, in remaining near their guns till after dark and then bringing them in. Lieutenant S.J.Stotesbury was acting as Staff Officer to me during the operation and was of the greatest assistance.

I also desire to bring to your notice the gallantry and devotion to duty shewn by Corporal Squance, who went out at 4.15 pm. during a very heavy bombardment and again about 10 pm, also under fire to repair the telephone wire from my H.Qrs. to the Firing Line.

Our casualties yesterday were 7 Officers and 155 Other Ranks, approximately. I consider that as the casualties during the recent operations are approaching 50% of our trench strength, an opportunity should be taken, as soon as possible, to give the time necessary for a complete reorganisation.

20.7.16.   (Signed) J.A.Tupman Lt.Col.
                                Comdg. 2/4th Glostershire Regt.

"A" Form.　　　　　　　　　　　　　　　Army Form C. 2121.

MESSAGES AND SIGNALS.

No. of Message

Prefix　Code　m.　Words　Charge　　This message is on a/c of:　　Recd. at　　m.

Office of Origin and Service Instructions.　　　　　　　　　　　　　　　　Service.　　Date

Confidential　　　Sent At　m. To　　　　　　　　　　　　　　　　　　　　From

By　　(Signature of "Franking Officer.")　　By

TO　183 Bde

HEADQUARTERS
No. BM 65
Date 4.9.16
183RD INFANTRY BRIGADE

Sender's Number　　Day of Month　　In reply to Number

* DG 535　　　　4th　　　　　　　　　　　　　　　　　　　　　　　　AAA

Attached please see account of Operations of the 19th July 1916 by Lt Col Commanding, in duplicate, for attachment to War Diary forwarded to you at the end of that month.

Please see my note in last column of Diary referred to.

From　2/4 Gloster

Place

Time

The above may be forwarded as now corrected.　(Z)　H.L. Hamsley

Censor.　Signature of Addressor or person authorised to telegraph in his name.

* This line should be erased if not required.

(4198) Wt. W14 42—M44. 300000 Pads. 12/15. Sir J. C. & S.

"C" Form (Duplicate).
MESSAGES AND SIGNALS.

Army Form C. 2123.

Str N6 pn 35

N C
Spr Simmons

Office Stamp.
LB
6.7.16

Handed in at N B ... Office ... m. Received 9.12 ... m.

TO   L B

Sender's Number	Day of Month	In reply to Number	AAA
BM 181	6th		

The corps commander has desired me to convey to the 2/4th Gloucesters and 2/4th Worcesters his congratulations on their having entered the enemy's trenches on the night of 4/5 July.

FROM
PLACE & TIME   N. C

5.7.16.

Dear Tupman

It gives me the
greatest pleasure to forward
this from the G.O.C.

I desire to add my sincere
congratulations; I only
grieve greatly that we have
lost poor Hannam &
other gallant fellows.

I will thank the G.O.C.
for his message.

Yrs. sincerely
C E Stewart

CONFIDENTIAL.

G.O.C.,
183 Inf. Bde.

Please convey to O.C., 2/4th Glosters my hearty appreciation of the gallant work of last night. From the reports I have received I consider that all ranks of the Company concerned acted with great courage and determination in carrying out a difficult enterprise and though we have had casualties they are out of all proportion to the effect which this attack must have on the enemy's morale, apart from the actual losses which he has actually suffered.

Major-General,
Commanding, 61 Div.

5.7.16.

2 Raids were carried out last night.

At 10.30 p.m. one company 2/7 Worcesters left their trenches, and raided the enemy's line via gap N.19.a.6±.9; they were delayed by finding some low concealed wire uncut, and by the ditch in front of the parapet being full of mud and water. Through this obstacle the men helped each other under a heavy fire of bombs, and entering enemy's trenches bombed right and left, one party penetrating 50 to 40 yards, and clearing several dugouts full of Germans. The party returned at 11.30 p.m. 2 Lewis guns which accompanied the party returned safely.

At 12.40 a.m. one company of 2/4 Glosters left their trenches, and at 1.10 a.m. advanced. They found the wire well cut about N.14.c.4.8, and entered the German trenches. Owing to the narrowness of the gap the rear of the company was blocked in the open for some time. Several dugouts were cleared, and it is thought that heavy casualties were inflicted on the enemy.

In both cases enemy's artillery fired heavily, but at the wrong places, and there was surprisingly little machine gun fire throughout the operations. The first parties of each raid reached enemys wire without casualties. The enemy's tactics appear to have been to block their trenches at each end of the gaps, and prepare bombing posts behind the parados.

The casualties inflicted on the enemy by the two raiding parties are estimated at 40 to 60 killed. All our killed and wounded were brought back.

5.7.16.

183 BRIGADE.

I have to report with reference to the raid carried out by my Battn. last night that the Company under the Command of Capt. F.J. Hanham left our Trenches at 12.40 a.m. and gained the enemy's parapet at 1.20 a.m. without drawing fire to any extent. only two men being wounded by bullets on the way over. Captain Hanham led the bombing parties into the enemys parapet through the wire which was well cut, with the greatest gallantry in the face of bombs and Machine Gun fire which was opened as our parties reached the wire. Captain Hanham cleared one bay with his revolver and a fierce bomb fight occured which I could see from where I was and during which, all there agree, 15 to 20 Germans were killed.

At about 1.30. Captain Hanham was hit in the leg with a bullet and had to be carried out by Pte. May and Pte. Allen.

Liet. F.A. Ridler who had gained the parapet by this time then assumed command and at about 1.35.a.m. found it impossible to maintain his hold on the breach. Srgt. Hyde and Pte. Godwin Cox and Franklin who had also gained the trench being either killed or taken prisoner.

The following also gained the trench, Pte Pearce and Pte Millard and escaped unwounded, L/Cpl. Hill and Pte Everett also got into the trench but were wounded. Lt. Ridler also reports the excellent work done by Pte Hudd who was seen to bayonet a German and take on three more single handed, he escaped unwounded but was wounded on the way back.

The other two platoon Officers 2/ Lt. E.O. Jago and 2/ Lt. O.A. Williamson were outside the wire endeavouring to keep the men together and encouraging them in every way possible. Severe casualties occurred on the way back. Lt. Ridler and Pte Allen and Pte Tone did not return to our lines till about 3 and until all wounded men had been brought in.

The 4 Company Stretcher bearers did excellent work in assisting with the wounded in " NO MAN'S LAND" of thoses Pte Nash did particular good work in bringing in the wounded.

Pte Newbery also behaved with great coolness on the German parapet with Lt. Ridler and brought in two wounded men himself.

Pte Martin also assisted Lt. Ridler to bring in one wounded man as did also Pte Coulston.

The Company Sergeant Major Peart who was with Captain Hanham carried a wounded man on his back for about 30 yards when the man on his back was killed. Sgt Majot Peart was afterwards hit in the heal. This raid was performed after a heavy bombardment or our trenches by the Germans.

I desire to recommend Captain Frederick J Hanham who died from his wound soon after reaching our trenches for the Victoria Cross as it was undoubtedly due to his splendid dash and courage and noble example that our party reached the enemy's parapet.

I wish to recommend 2/Lieut. Frederick Arnold Didler 2/4 Glosters for the Military Cross for his ably seconding his Company Commander and his loyalty and devotion to his men in remaining out until all the wounded had been brought in. He showed a splendid example of what an Officer should be.

I also desire to recommend the following for a Military award.

2568	Compy. Sgt. Major	William S. Peart	2/4 Glosters
3543	Pte.	Jack Rudd	do
3324	"	Henry May	do
3885	Drummer	Edward Newberry	do
3377	A/ Lce. Cpl	Arthur Hill	do.
6251	Pte	Leonard Everett	do.
6248	Pte	Harold Allen	do.
4259	Pte	William James True	do.
5165	Pte	John James Nash	do.

The strength of raiding party was 4 Officers and 138 O.R. not including an R.E. party of 2 N.C.Os. and 4 men.

                                           (sgd) J.A. Tupman Lt. Col.
5. 7. 16.   O.C. 2/4 Glosters.

The casualties in raid were:-

        Captain Frank J. Hannam Wounded (died of wounds)
        2/ Lt. O. Allison Williamson Wounded.

        Other Ranks.   Killed 2. Wounded 28.
                                Missing 8. Shock. 1.

CONFIDENTIAL: SECRET

61st Division No. Q 36

D. A. G.,
    3rd Echelon,
        Base.

- - - - - - - -

The attached account of operations on the 19th July, 1916, is forwarded for attachment to the War Diary of the 2/4th Glosters - forwarded to you under my Q 36 of the 5th ult.

D. H. Q.,
5th September, 1916.

for Major-General,
Commanding 61st Division.

The O C 2/1th Glosters
─────────────

I was present on the raid of the 5th inst, and I saw Capt. F J Hannam leading his men in a most gallant manner in the face of bombs and machine gun fire.

He repeatedly encouraged his men and when on the German parapet he cleared a bay full of Germans with his revolver, besides throwing bombs which caused many casualties

After he was wounded he still continued to encourage the men but had to be taken back owing to loss of blood

F A Ridler 2/Lieut
2/1th Gloucester Regt.
8/7/16

The O.C. 2/4 Gloucesters,

I was present on the raid of the 5th July 1916 and I saw Captain Hannam 2/4 Gloucesters leading his men the whole way across. When our Artillery barrage lifted, he was the first to rise up and go through the gap in the German wire onto their parapet. I heard him encouraging his men to follow. The last I saw of him was when he was firing his revolver into the German trench.

P. O. Jogo
2/Lt 2/4 Gloucesters

8/7/16

"A" Form.
Army Form C. 2121.
MESSAGES AND SIGNALS.

TO: 61 Div.

Sender's Number: G.535.
Day of Month: 12/7.

The Corps Commander realises now that the full report of the raids on 4/5 July carried out by 7th Worcesters and 4th Glosters has been received that they were far more successful was at first believed He wishes you to congratulate these two battalions on the success of their operations.

From: Eleventh Corps.
Time: 2.50 p.m.

7/4 Glosters
7/7 Worcesters ✓

Forwarded.

BHQ
13.7.16.
Brigade Major, 183rd Infantry Brigade

DIVISION ROUTINE ORDERS by

MAJOR General Colin Mackenzie C.B.

Commanding 61st Division.

Headquarters,
29th July 1916.

222. **AWARDS FOR GALLANTRY.**

The following awards for gallantry have been made:

MILITARY CROSS.

Lieut. Frederick Arnold Ridler, 2/4Bn. The Gloucestershire Regiment T.F.

For gallantry and ability displayed during a raid at FAUQUISSART on the night of the 4/5th July. He assumed command when Captain Hannam was mortally wounded, and it was due to his skilful handling that the operation was completed successfully, and the troops withdrawn steadily and in good order to our own trenches.

Notes for C. Coy.

1. Point a point of Exit from our trenches
2. Whether our wire requires cutting
3. Forming up place if any in no man's land.
4. Point of assault.
5. Guides to lead to point in 4.
6. No. of Parties.
   This would appear to be 4. One for each corner of trenches to be held.
   Each party would be responsible for taking and holding its own corner and also for joining up with parties in the two adjacent corners who should meet ½ way.
7. One bombing party of 10rcs & 8 to be told off to bomb down & barricade Enemy's trench running into each corner.
   to be followed by a consolidation party of 5 men with sandbags (50) and 1 pick & 4 shovels.
8. Party of 12 .... to clear dug outs in front line and meet party from the other end.
   No bombs should be thrown by these parties except into dugouts which after being bombed are to be cleared immediately after the explosion with the bayonet.
9. Party from each corner in support line to work inwards clearing any dugouts in support line
10. Parties in similar manner to work back from Support line to Fire Trench.
11. One officer to be told off to superintend the work at each corner.
12. As soon as the area is cleared of enemy every effort must be made to get fire position to repel counter attack and to deal with any parties of the enemy who may attempt to come down the Commn. trenches or over the open.
13. Parties at corners of Support line must be prepared to bring a cross fire to bear across their front or to beat off an attack made on the corners

14. Every effort is to be made to obtain identification of Germans in occupation by cutting off shoulder badges etc.

Artillery

15. The artillery will bombard (the wire having been cut previously) from 0.0. to 0.30.
At 0.30. The Artillery will lift and place a barrage behind the selected area and on each side of it.
The Company will assault.
The Barrage will be continued until 1.30 and then cease till 1.32. which will be the signal for the Company to withdraw.
At 1.32. ⅓ʳᵈ of the Artillery will be directed against the enemy's parapet to the right and ⅓ to the left. of the selected area in order to cover the ~~retirement~~ withdrawal. While the remaining ⅓ʳᵈ Artillery will continue the barrage beyond the enemy's Support line.

M.G.

16. Machine Guns will cooperate with the Artillery and place a barrage in conjunction with the Artillery and on the same areas.

17. The Artillery and M.G. fire will cease on the Company returning to our own line.

18. There must be no firing up or down trenches in the area — bayonet only, and bombs for dugouts.

19. The parties for the Support line will assault first and immediately proceed to the corners of Support line — closely followed over the parapet by the parties for the Fire line.

20. The party for Support line must be prepared to cut wire in front of enemy's trench if this is not already done.

21. A small party of R.E. with explosives will accompany one of the Fire line parties to demolish Cable or any mortar found in the area that is too heavy to carry away.

22. Bomb dumps will be formed at the corners of the area. Also in our own fire line near the point or points of exit.

23. All men will rifles will carry 120 rds ammn. An ammn dump will also be formed near point of exit in our own line.

24. The Company Stretcher Bearers will accompany the parties to the enemy fire line. The M.O. and a special party to be ready in our own fire line at an advanced dressing station — to be arranged.

25. One Lewis gun will be told off to sweep No Mans Land on either flank to prevent any parties of the enemy getting between our raiding party and our line.

26. The withdrawal will be conducted as follows. First the support line — all men closing on their own corner and passing down the corner trench as rapidly as possible. The last men to withdraw being the bombers.
When the support line parties are over the parapet the fire line parties will follow in like manner.
The A. N. Co. with a selected private will be detailed to see the trenches clear before withdrawing and report to the officer of the party at each corner who will accompany the last of the party.

27. A succession of short flashes in torch will mean.

Platoons will average 35 and be disposed as follows:-

Fire line.
a. Bombing Party.   1. N.C.O. & 8. men.   60
⊕ b. Consolidating do.   1 — 5 —   15
c. Clearing party to   } 2 — 10.   25
   work onwards.
✱ d. To hold corner.   1 — 4ˣ   10
✝ e. Runners.   — — 2 —   20
f. To superintend.   1. Officer.   ———
                                                190
                          1 — 5 — 29 = 35.

Support line.
(a). Bombing Party.   1 — 8
⊕ (b) Consolidating —   1 — 5
c. Clearing Party to   1 — 5
   work onwards.
d. do to work down   1 — 5
   Support trench to F.L.
✱ e. To hold corner.   1 — 4ˣ
✝ f. Runners.   2.
g. Officer.   1 —
                          ——————————————
                          1 — 5 — 29 = 35.

ˣ These carry wire cutters.
⊕ Carry 10 sandbags each. and 1 pick & 3 shovels with party.
✱ Every one carries 2 bombs and except bombers.
   wear equipment less pack. haversack. waterbottle
   entrenching tool.
✝ Runners carry 2 bucket of bombs each.

Bar 45

Willow

SB.

Brown Earth   Stratus   Brown Earth

Bar 34

Bar 45
140

Vol 4

CONFIDENTIAL

WAR DIARY OF

2/4TH BATTALION GLOUCESTERSHIRE REGIMENT.

FROM 1ST AUGUST 1916 TO 31ST AUGUST 1916.

VOLUME I

Army Form C. 2118.

WAR DIARY
INTELLIGENCE SUMMARY

(Erase heading not required.)

2/4th Batt Gloster Regt

Instructions regarding War Diaries and Intelligence Summaries are contained in F.S. Regs., Part II. and the Staff Manual respectively. Title Pages will be prepared in manuscript.

Place	Date	Hour	Summary of Events and Information	Remarks and references to Appendices
FAUQUISSART (Left Sub Sec.)	Aug 1	5 am	Relief by 1/6 Glosters commenced	
		10.15 am	Relief Complete	
LAVENTIE	" 2		Battalion moved into Billets — D Coy to Posts nr Moats:- DEAD END, PICANTIN, J'NOUGOMONT.	
			Company Training. Fatigues	
"	" 3		do	
"	" 4	3 pm	Lecture to Officers & NCOs "The Spirit of the Bayonet" by Major Campbell, Gordon Hrs.	
"	" 5		Company Training. Fatigues	
"		12 noon	Relief by 1/6 Glosters commenced	
FAUQUISSART (Left Sub Sec.)		3.35 pm	Relief complete. Casualties:- Wounded 1 Rank.	
"	" 6	5.45 am	G.O.C. Div called at H.Qrs. Casualties:- Killed 1 Or. Wounded 5 Or.	
"	" 7		Draft of 48 Ors. arrived	
"	" 8		Day quiet. Casualties:- Wounded 3 Or.	
"	" 9		Relief by 2/4 Oxford & Bucks L.I.	
		4.30 pm	Relief Complete. Casualties: Killed 3 Or. Wounded 3 Or.	
LA GORGUE		8.15 pm	Battalion marched into Billets. Billeting Complete	

Army Form C. 2118.

WAR DIARY
INTELLIGENCE SUMMARY
2/4 Batt Gloster R.

(Erase heading not required.)

Place	Date	Hour	Summary of Events and Information	Remarks and references to Appendices
LA GORGUE	Aug 10		Kit Inspection & Refitting. Bathing	
"	" 11		Company Training	
"	" 12	3pm	do	
			Medical Inspection.	
			A.P.M's Inspection of Transport &c	
"	" 13		Range Practice	
"	" 14		Company Training	
"	" 15		183rd Bde Horse Show	
"	" 16		Company Training	
"	" 17		do	
CROIX BARBEE (NEUVE CHAPELLE SECTION)	" 18	2pm	Battalion relieved march out. Billets vacated by 1/7th Regt 94 Bde. A Coy relieved Pts as follows :- LORETTO, EUSTON, RUE du PUITS, & CROIX MARMES	
		2.5pm	Relief complete	
		5pm	Battalion Complete	

Army Form C. 2118.

WAR DIARY
or
INTELLIGENCE SUMMARY
(Erase heading not required.)

2/4th York R

Instructions regarding War Diaries and Intelligence Summaries are contained in F. S. Regs., Part II. and the Staff Manual respectively. Title Pages will be prepared in manuscript.

Place	Date	Hour	Summary of Events and Information	Remarks and references to Appendices
CROIX-BARBEE	Aug 19		Company Training. Fatigues. Adjts' meeting at Bde Hqrs.	
"	" 20		Church Parade. Fatigues.	
"	" 21		Fatigues	
NEUVE CHAPELLE Left Sub Section	" 22	12 noon	Relief of 1/6 Glosters in Left Sub Section commenced. C & D Coys in Front Line. A Coy in posts (Port Arthur + Mills) & "B" in reserve. Casualties: wounded 2 O.R.	
		4 pm	Relief complete	
	" 23	(evening)	Bombardment by our H.T.M.s.	
	" 24	"	Raid by 1/8 R. Warwicks, on our left.	
	" 25	"	2nd day Intermittent Artillery activity. Casualties:- Wounded 2/Lt E. H. PARSONS.	
	" 26	3.45 pm	Relief by 12th York & Lancaster Regt. Posts relieved by 13 Y & L. R. Casualties: wounded 2/Lt E. TANNER + 1 O.R. Killed 1 O.R.	
RIEZ BAILLEUL		6.30 pm	Battalion moved into Billets. Billetting complete	

Army Form C. 2118.

3/4 R 9/oks R

WAR DIARY
INTELLIGENCE SUMMARY
(Erase heading not required.)

Instructions regarding War Diaries and Intelligence Summaries are contained in F.S. Regs., Part II. and the Staff Manual respectively. Title pages will be prepared in manuscript.

Place	Date	Hour	Summary of Events and Information	Remarks and references to Appendices
RIEZ BAILLEUL	Aug 27		Church Parade. Kit Inspections	
"	Aug 28		Fatigues - Bathing & Medical Inspection (C+D Coys)	
"	Aug 29		Fatigues. Range practice (Snipers) Bombing (C+D Coys) Medical Inspection A+B Coys. Heavy Rain.	
"	Aug 30		Tuesday. Football. Heavy Rain	
"	Aug 31		Fatigues. Bathing C+D Coys. Bombing B Coy.	

R S Oulton
Lt Col.
Commdg. 3/4 9/okr R.

Vol 5

G.5

CONFIDENTIAL.

WAR DIARY OF

2/4th BATTALION GLOUCESTERSHIRE REGIMENT.

FROM 1ST SEPTEMBER 1916 TO 30TH SEPTEMBER 1916

VOLUME 5.

Army Form C. 2118.

WAR DIARY
or
INTELLIGENCE SUMMARY
(Erase heading not required.)

2/4 Batt Gloster Regt.

SEPTEMBER 1916

Instructions regarding War Diaries and Intelligence Summaries are contained in F.S. Regs., Part II. and the Staff Manual respectively. Title Pages will be prepared in manuscript.

Place	Date	Hour	Summary of Events and Information	Remarks and references to Appendices
MOATED GRANGE SECN.	1-9-16		W/O.R.T Regt reorganised from sick leave in England. Relief of 7/6th Glosters in Left Sub Section. Following Posts taken over :- WINCHESTER, TILLELOY N, DREADNAUGHT & GRANTS.	
do.	2-9-16	3.30pm	Relief complete. Quiet day.	
do.	3-9-16		Trenches M 35 & 6.6 to M 29 d 9.7.8. taken over by 1/5th Worcesters. Trenches M 24 c 6.1 to ERITH ST (inclus), also ERITH POST, taken over from 1/5 Gloster. Relief Complete. Wet day. Casualties :- Wounded 1 O/rank.	
do.	4-9-16	12.30pm	Wet day. Casualties :- Wounded 1 O/rank.	
do.	5-9-16		Bombardment by our MTH S.	
do.	6-9-16	4pm	Raid by 2/Lt COGHLAN & 10 O/rank. C Coy. Not successful owing to non explosion of Bangalore Torpedo. Party returned in safety. Casualties :- Wounded 1 O/rank.	
do.	7-9-16	9am	Relief by 2/6th Glosters Commenced.	
		4.15pm	Relief complete. Battalion moved into Billets.	
RIEZ BAILLEUL		7pm	Billets Complete. Following Posts taken over from 2/7 Worcesters :- LONELY, MIN, ROUGE CROIX E, ROUGE CROIX N, LA NASSEE, PONT DU HEM, LA FLINQUE, HARROW, ETON & CHARTER HOUSE. (Total Garrisons :- 10 NCOs & 46 men)	

WAR DIARY
or
INTELLIGENCE SUMMARY

2/4th Glosk R.
Ita

Army Form C. 2118.

Place	Date	Hour	Summary of Events and Information	Remarks and references to Appendices
RIEZ BAILLEUL	8-9-16		Battalion Clothing & rifle Insp. Bathing. NCO D Corps & HqD. Fatigues.	
do.	9-9-16		"Fun Day" Football Concert.	
do.	10.9.16		Church Parade.	
do.	11-9-16	10.30 am	Battalion moved into Billets vacated by 1st Oxfords.	
S ROBERMETZ				
do.	12-9-16		Company Training.	
do.	13.9.16		do -	
do.	14.9.16		Range Practice at LE SART.	
do.	15-9-16		Company Training.	
BOUTDEVILLE	16-9-16	2.15 pm	Battalion march out Billets.	
		5.7 pm	Billeting complete. A Coy till new RUE du PUITS Patl. (1 NCO & 3 men)	
do.	17-9-16		Church Parade. Bathing HQrs.	
do.	18.9.16		Company Training. Hot Day. Bathing NCO & Corps. B Coy Nth on Artillery Posts — WELLINGTON, HUIT MAISONS N. and S.	
do.	19-9-16		Company Training Hot Day.	

WAR DIARY
INTELLIGENCE SUMMARY

Army Form C. 2118.

1/4 Gloster Regt.

Place	Date	Hour	Summary of Events and Information	Remarks and references to Appendices
NEUVE CHAPELLE SECTION	20/9/16	3.45pm	Relief of 1/6 Glosters in left Sub Section 4th Army. Posts Ashurnerie:- CHATEAU, CHURCH & QUEZON. Relief complete. B.H.Q. Coys in Front Line. C & D Coys in "B" Line.	
do.	21.9.16		Hot Day	
do.	22.9.16		Bombarded by enemy F.T.M.s & M.T.M.s.	
do.	23.9.16	11.30pm	Inspection of Bomb Charges - Bomb C and Bomb D vice versa. Casualties - Accidentally Wounded - 10 Ranks. Wounded - 2 Ranks. Complete.	
do.	24.9.16		LT.M. & M.T.M. shoot. Casualties - Wounded 3 Ranks.	
do.	25.9.16	9.45am.	"C" Coy. H.Qrs. moved from Front line to HUSH HALL. Move complete. Raid by 9/14 CUMMING & 14 Ranks. Party failed to get Bangalore Torpedo sufficiently far into German wire to explode, but bombed their Trenches & returned under heavy fire. All returned safely. Casualties:- Wounded 1 Rank.	
do.	26.9.16	3.45pm	Relief by 1/6 Glosters. Relief complete.	
BOIS DENULE	"		Battalion moved into Billets.	
do.	27.9.16		Battery Clothing & Refitting. Medical Inspection C & D Coys.	
do.	28.9.16		Coy. Training. Fatigues. Medical Inspection A & B Coys & Hqrs.	
do.	29.9.16		Coy. Training.	
do.	30.9.16		Coy. Training. Special Demonstration of "Flammenwerfer".	

J A Tupman
Comdg. 1/4 Glosters
30/9/16

From O.C. Coy
2/4th Gloucester Regt

To O.C.
2/4th Gloucester Regt

24.9.16

It is proposed to raid the enemy's trenches tonight at a point M.35.d.9.3½. Will you please arrange for R.E. cooperation with a Bangalore Torpedo and also for the Artillery to stand by ready to barrage the enemy support & communication trenches on the message BARRAGE being sent to G.H. Could I possibly have 2 batteries ready to help please? I don't want any preliminary bombardment.

Re the Bangalore, if it could be arranged for the torpedo to be placed in position by R.E's and exploded from NO MANS LAND

from a position close to the
O/C Stand, this would be a
"great help".

May we have another look at
the aeroplane maps, too?

Tonic will be notified later
by CODE under message BING

[signature]
O/C O Coy

From O.C. Coy
2/4 Gloucester Regt
To O.C.
2/4th Gloucester Regt

24 - 9 - 16

Refree proposed operations tonight. It is intended to leave these trenches at 9:30 pm and explode at 10 pm. Will you please warn Bastns on flanks.

We shall require 2 signallers detailed, preferably other than those who went last time, and two extra phones.

I hope it will be possible to explode the torpedo from NO MANS LAND this time.

[signature] Capt.
O.C. Coy

SECRET.

183ᵈ Bde.

I beg to submit following proposals for raid by C Coy tomorrow night, 25ᵗʰ inst.

1. Party to leave our Trenches 9.30 p.m.

2. Bangalore Torpedo to be exploded 10 p.m.

3. Reference 2 above. O/c C Coy has expressed a special wish that this may be done from NO MAN'S LAND. and not from our Trenches.

I should be very glad if arrangements could be made for this.

L. G. Brinsley, for O/c

24/9/16

From. O.C. Coy
    2/4th Gloucester Regt
To. O.C.
    2/4th Gloucester Regt.

25.9.16

Reference tonight's operations:-
The raiding party, which will consist of 2/Lt Cummins & 14 O/R will leave by 35 2 at 9.30 p.m. They will endeavour to place B.T. in position by 10 p.m. when the explosion is timed for. I hope that the R.E. officer who will explode the pipe will accompany the party up to this point and return after explosion has taken place. The raiding party will then endeavour to enter and bomb the enemy front line trenches for five minutes. A code word to retire has been arranged. A covering party consisting 2/Lt Coghlan

a Lewis gun & 15 O/R will stand by ready to go to the assistance of the raiding party if needed.

Will you please arrange for two signallers to accompany the party and 2 extra phones with 400 yds of wire. They should report here at 8 pm, please.

Also, may we have 2 "Batteries standing by" to form a "pocket barrage" round the point of entry at M 35 d 9. 3½ on the message BARRAGE being sent to GA. This is in case of counter attack.

I have consulted the MO and he suggests that the Cpl and another RAMC man with the Bn should be sent to the Coy as dressers for the night. Can this be arranged, please?

Code attached.

J.S. Wynter Capt
O/C C Coy

CODE

BING = Raiding Party Started
AAA   = Half way across.
BBB   = Arrived outside the wire
CCC   = Bangalore in Position.
BURST = Bangalore exploded.
RATS = Coming home.
TWEED = Raiding Party all in.

BARRAGE sent to GA =
"Pocket Barrage" around
N 35 d 9. 3½.

25. 9. 16

SECRET

To:-
No 2 Field Co R.E.
4 Glosters (for information)

[Stamp: HEADQUARTERS No S.175 Date 25.9.16 183 INFANTRY BRIGADE]

Please supply O.C. 4th Glosters with one 76 ft. Bangalore Torpedo and all necessary parts by 6 p.m. this evening. Please give him all the help you can and if he requires it, a man to help explode the Torpedo.

M. M. Pangfor
Captain
Bde Major 183 Inf Bde

Bde H.Q.
25/9/16

"C" Form (Duplicate).
MESSAGES AND SIGNALS.

Army Form C. 2123.
(In books of 50's in duplicate.)

No. of Message ....

· 1. FCD 13   PC.
              Petithez

Charges to Pay.
£   s.   d.

Office Stamp.
CB
25/9/16

Service Instructions.
PC

Handed in at .... Office .... m. Received 7 ..m.

TO   GB.

Sender's Number	Day of Month	In reply to Number	AAA
RP8	25		
FLITTED to FRONT LINE TILL PUM			
		RAID 25.9.16	

FROM PLACE & TIME   PC   6.55 p

VERY SECRET.   Copy No. 1.

1.   4th GLOSTERS intend to explode a Bangalore Torpedo
at M.35.d.9.3½. about 10 pm tonight, and a small party
will try and enter the enemy trenches.

2.   Right Group, R.F.A. will arrange to form a Barrage
with 2 Batteries round the point of entry, if required.
The Artillery Liaison Officer will call direct on the
Batteries for this Barrage at the request of the Infantry

3.   If the Barrage is called for, the L.T.M's will create
a diversion by firing heavily on the enemy front line
from S.5.b.5.2. to S.5.b.8.6.
        The Machine Guns will also search C.T's just N. and
S. of the BOIS du BIEZ.

4.   O.C.M.G.Coy, and T.M.B. will report at H.Q. 4th
GLOSTERS at 5 pm today to arrange for communication
in case the Barrage is called for.

        ACKNOWLEDGE.

                                        Captain,
                                    Brigade Major.
                                 183rd Infantry Bde.

Copy No. 1 - 4th Glosters.
  "   2 - 8th Worcesters.
  "   3 - Right Group, R.F.A.
  "   4 - 183 L.T.M.Battery.
  "   5 - 183 M.G.Coy.
  "   6 - File.

N. Secret

HEADQUARTERS
No. S. 175
Date 25-9-16
188th INFANTRY BRIGADE

O.C. 4th Glosters.

Herewith diagram showing
arrangements for barrage
for tonight, if it is
called for.

The Artillery are sending
you two Liaison officers
tonight. 1 for Bn HQ
1 for Coy HQ.

I hope this will prove
satisfactory.

25-9-16

Ughs Pang. from Capt
Bry Major. 188 Bde

25/9/16

Barrage if required

A/307

B/307

"C" Form (Duplicate).
MESSAGES AND SIGNALS.

Army Form C. 2123.
(In books of 50's in duplicate.)
No. of Message............

	Charges to Pay.	Office Stamp.
SM 1Bay Ly 3DO M Baillle/W	£ s. d.	BDP 27/7/16
Service Instructions.		

Handed in at....**BDO**....Office....9..m. Received....9.30..m.

TO   **BDO**

Sender's Number	Day of Month	In reply to Number	A A A
SC1669	27th		

Division wire begins aaa
D A G base wire
begins aaa A Q
1405 26 aaa Send
following report to O C
reinforcements ROUEN aaa age
under 18 aaa 44 Pte
A E BEVIS BDP aaa Ends aaa
Report departure by wire to
this office

20/7 to headrs A D Coy

FROM
PLACE & TIME   **BDO**

G.6

Vol 6

CONFIDENTIAL

WAR DIARY

OF

2/4th BATTALION GLOUCESTERSHIRE REGT

FROM OCTOBER 1st 1916
TO OCTOBER 31st 1916

VOLUME 5

WAR DIARY or INTELLIGENCE SUMMARY

Army Form C. 2118.

(Erase heading not required.)

Place	Date	Hour	Summary of Events and Information	Remarks and references to Appendices
BOUT DE VILLE	Oct 1		Church Parade	
	Oct 2		B⁰ relieved 2/6th q[uarte]rs in left sub-section NEUVE CHAPELLE – Relief complete 3.30 p.m. 1 Officer & 2 O.R. arrived for attachment for instruction.	B Coy 2/6 relieves B Coy A " A " C " C " A " D "
	3rd		Wet day. 1 O.R. wounded	1 O.R. wounded, died of wounds same day.
	4th		Lt. Col. TUPMAN proceeded to B.de as a/Brigadier.	
	5th		Fine day. Dispositions of Coys changed, B changing over with C, and A with D.	
	6th		Cloudy. Usual T.M. shoots. Enemy M.G. more active than usual.	
	7th		Showery. Orders for relief received.	
	8th		Relieved by 2/6th q[uarte]rs. {D Coy relieved by A Coy 2/6 q[uarte]rs C " C B " B A " D} Relief complete 3.20 P.M. B⁰ moved into billets at BOUT DE VILLE. Billeting complete 6.30 p.m.	
	9th		Clothing and refitting. Bathing, all Coys and H.Q.	
	10th		Training: medical inspection of Transport and Q.M. staff	
	11th		Training: meeting of Adj⁴, Transport officers & R.M. at Bde H.Q. Capt. D.C. BARNSLEY proceeded to England for C.O.'s course. Lt JESSOP temporarily took over these duties of Adjutant.	
	12th		Training	
	13th		Training – kit inspection – 50 O.R. reinforcements arrived. Relieved 2/6 q[uarte]rs in left sub-section NEUVE CHAPELLE. Dispositions D – B – A. Relief C	
	14th		complete 3.4 p.m. – 6th Bavarian Division opposite to us.	

WAR DIARY / INTELLIGENCE SUMMARY

Army Form C. 2118.

Place	Date	Hour	Summary of Events and Information	Remarks and references to Appendices
	Oct 15th		Cloudy. usual T.M. shoots. Capt Daniell 3/3 Rif Detl attached for instruction. Draft of 34 O.R. arrived LA GORGUE 5·30 pm. 2 O.R. wounded by splinters of one of our shells which burst in enemy line.	
	Oct 16th		Lt. Col. TUPMAN returned from B.de and took over command. Draft joined the Battalion in the line. 1 O.R. killed. 3 O.R. wounded.	
	Oct 17th		Capt Daniell posted to C. Coy. Lieut. Riddle proceeded to Bde as Intelligence Officer vice Lt. Attenpt (in turn). Lecture at LAVENTIE by Major-General STEVENS commanding 5th Division. Summary of experience of Pri Green, LTM Battery taken. Captain Pratt killed, Lieuts OWEN and C.H. Pritchard wounded (all by one aerial torpedo). Later Owen died of wounds. Major Bowden proceeded to GAS SCHOOL. Lecture on "SOMME FIGHTING" at LAVENTIE.	
	Oct 18th		Very hot – draft of 100 arrived.	
	Oct 19th		Still wet and colder.	
	Oct 20th		Relieved by 2/6th Glosters: (A Coy relieved by D Coy 2/6th Glosters arriving ambulant 3·45 pm B : : : : : : : : Bn Pershed to billets at – C : : : : : : : BOUT DE VILLE	
	Oct 21st		L.G., Bombers and Snipers demonstration at Divl training school, LE DRUMEZ. B2 found guard of honour for Medal presentation by Corps Commander at LA GORGUE. Draft of 34 O.R. arrived. B.G.C. inspects new drafts. A Coy rejoined.	
	Oct 22nd		Lt. S.J. STOTESBURY returned from 1st Army School, CONDETTE, and took over duties of Adjutant. Refitting and bathing. Party of ARTISTS RIFLES returned to unit.	
	Oct 23rd		Bn inspected by Brigadier in column of route on RUE DU POUCH; head of column at R.16. C.7.3.	
	Oct 24th		(Sheet 36A) Lecture to A, C, & D Coys by an N.C.O. from Divl Gas School.	

WAR DIARY
or
INTELLIGENCE SUMMARY
(Erase heading not required.)

Army Form C. 2118.

Place	Date	Hour	Summary of Events and Information	Remarks and references to Appendices

	Oct 25th		Relieved 4/5 B⁰ Glos Regt in left sub-section NEUVE CHAPELLE. Dispositions:-
			     A B C
			   Supp + CHATEAU Gds + CHURCH right + HILLS
			               D
			           B line and EUSTON
			 Relief complete 3.50 p.m. Wet day.	

	Oct 26th		Quiet day.	
	Oct 27th		Quiet day. Line reconnoitred by O.C. and O.C. Coys Q.V.R. 1/9th London.	
	Oct 28th		Relieved in trenches by Q.V.R. relief complete 3.57 p.m. (A Coy ½ls relieved by A Coy Q.V.R. Wet day. Capt DANIELL left with advance unit. B⁰ went B " " B " into billets at BOUT DEVILLE. 18.32 Bde HQ closed at C " " C " LES HUIT MAISONS R.29.d (not sheet 36 A) at 3.30 p.m and D " " D " opened at BUSNES P.31 & B8. at the same hour	
	Oct 29th		B⁰ relieved in billets at BOUT DEVILLE by Queens Westn. B⁰ marched to RUE L'ECLEME V.4 (Awt 36a). Billeting complete 4.15 p.m. 183rd Bde in Army reserve and ready to move at an hours notice up to midnight 29th/30th. Lt RIDLER rejoined B⁰'s LE HAG.G.ART rejoined B⁰'s temporarily. Wet day. Orders received for further move on Nov 1st	
	Oct 30th		Wet day.	
	Oct 31st		Coy and specialist training. Section of all officers by C.O. Company specialist training preparations for early move on following day. Church parade in afternoon.	

S/ S.G. ....
Lieut Col ....
2/4th Btn Gloucester Regt.

Confidential.
War Diary of
24th Bam. Ken. Regt. from
Nov. 1st 1916 to Nov. 30th 1916.

Volume

Army Form C. 2118.

WAR DIARY
or
INTELLIGENCE SUMMARY.
(Erase heading not required.)

Place	Date	Hour	Summary of Events and Information	Remarks and references to Appendices
In the field	1.11.16		Bn marched to BUCHEL, route L'ECLEME - BUSNETTES - BASRIEUX - BURBURE - RAIMBERT. Billeting complete 1715 f/m. Other ranks arrd in by L.G. billet.	
	3.11.16		Bn marched to OSTREVILLE, route CAUCHY - FLORINGHEM - PERNES - VALHUON - LATHIEULOYE. Bn march. 9/30 am, arr. 7th bn. Billeting complete 2115 f/m.	
	3.11.16		Bn marched to CHELERS area, route MARQUAY - BAILLEUL aux CORNAILLES. A & B Coy at CHELERS. C & D Coy & HQ at BAILLEUL. Bn had recompanies Bn on march. Billeting complete 1915 f/m. Company training.	
	4.11.16 5.11.16		Bn marched to BONEVILLE, route LIGNY ST. FOCHEL - TERNAS. Bn had accompanies Bn on march. Billeting complete 3 pm.	
	6.11.16		Bn marched to BURE AU BOIS, route SIBIVILLE - FREVENT - VACQUERIE - BOUQ. Bn march 9/30 am, arr 7th bn. Nil below. Billeting complete 2115 f/m. Very wet day. Company training nil day.	
	7.11.16 8.11.16 9.11.16		Company training 6 mis mtr f/v Coy commence training in Lewis gun. MG by Company. Specialist training. Bookmen coy arrangements. Party of officers N.C.O. attended demonstration of attacks of trenches by N.F.?	
	10.11.16		Bn discard practice	

T2131. Wt. W708—776. 500000. 4/15. Sir J. C. & S.

WAR DIARY
or
INTELLIGENCE SUMMARY

Army Form C. 2118.

Place	Date	Hour	Summary of Events and Information	Remarks and references to Appendices
In the field	11/11/16		Bde Staff rode to 2nd inf. Bde. & Bde commander attended by Divnl Commander. Fine day.	
	12/11/16		Bn tactical exercise for NCOs in morning. Church Parade afternoon. Fine day.	
	13/11/16		Bn tactical exercises & specialist training. Fine day.	
	14/11/16		Officer Staff rode. Practice advancing through wood lying up & bivouac, marching & light work. Digging strong pts under R.E. Fine day.	
	15/11/16		Bn marched to HEUZECOURT & GRIMONT, made AUXI-LE-CHATEAU – MAZICOURT – MONTIGNY les JONGLEURS. Billeting complete 3/30 pm.	
	16/11/16		Bn marched to FRANQUEVILLE, made BERNAVILLE – DOMESMONT. Billeting completed from Bn march brigade (two 7/6 bdes & 317 bdes) to LA VICOGNE, made DOMART – ST. LEGER – BERTEAUCOURT – HALLOYLES TERNOIS – HAVERNAS – NAOURS – TALMAS. Billeting complete 9 pm.	
	18/11/16		Bn marched to SENLIS, made HERISSART – CONTAY – WARLOY. Billeting complete 9/30 pm.	
	19/11/16		Bn marched to Huts etc. in MARTINSART WOOD, made SENLIS – BOUZINCOURT. Marching complete 17/30 pm. Fine cold day.	
	20/11/16		600 men (with officers) on fatigue parties from town to 11pm. Staff joined at midnight.	
	21/11/16		Fatigues as previous day.	
	22/11/16		Bn marched to ALBERT. Billeting complete 12 noon. Foggy day.	

WAR DIARY
or
INTELLIGENCE SUMMARY.
(Erase heading not required.)

Army Form C. 2118.

Place	Date	Hour	Summary of Events and Information	Remarks and references to Appendices
In the Trenches			Working party of 100 O.R. + off. from A Coy supplied. Route to MOUQUET FARM reconnoitred by 2/Lt Fleming. Rest of day quiet.	
	24/11/16		Working party of 100 O.R. + off. supplied. Raining.	
	25/11/16		Working party of 300 O.R. + off. supplied. Raining. Heavy enemy artillery fire. Attack practice. 1 off. arrived.	
	26/11/16		Bn. marched to MARTINSART WOOD. Heavy artillery fire J.35 and Thiepval.	
	27/11/16		C.O. reg't + Coy Commanders viewed the line. Working party of 200 O.R. supplied. 2/Lt + 8 Coy diggers practice.	
	28/11/16		Working party of 50 O.R. supplied. Digging practice + patrol scheme by Raleigh + Reading party of 250 O.R. supplied. 1 off. attended Hospital.	
	29/11/16		Relieved 4 Ox and Bucks in Left Subsector opposite GRANDCOURT. A Coy Front, B Left Front, C Reg't reserve, D Left support. Right Coy G.H.Q. 10.5 P.M.	
	30/11/16		Casualties 1 O.R. wounded.	

E.D. Mannsborough Lieut
a/adjt
2/4 Glos. Reg't

Vol 8

G.8

CONFIDENTIAL.

WAR DIARY.

2/4 GLOSTERS.

DECEMBER 1916.

CONFIDENTIAL.

WAR DIARY, VOL. 8

OF THE 2/4 BATT., THE GLOUCESTERSHIRE REG.

DECEMBER 1916.

WAR DIARY
or
INTELLIGENCE SUMMARY

(Erase heading not required.)

Army Form C. 2118.

Place	Date	Hour	Summary of Events and Information	Remarks and references to Appendices
	Dec 1		Intense bombardment by our artillery from 11.30 am to 12 noon to E enemy replied on HESSIAN, REGINA and DESIRE trenches, firing intermittently throughout the day. Weather cold and foggy. Work on improving trenches, drainage and burying dead. 1 O.R. wounded killed	
	2		Sharp frost and foggy in the morning: work of improving trenches and digging strong points continued. German M.G found by D Coy in an old dug-out in Stump Road. 1 O.R. wounded	
	3		Clear day - Usual artillery activity. Orders for relief received	
	4		Very clear day - useful information gained enemy artillery fairly active. 1 O.R. killed, 3 O.R. wounded	
	5		Relieved by 2/6 Gloster's A+B and HQ proceed to AVELUY SIDING huts, C and D Coys to reserve trenches near MOUQUET FARM. Enemy artillery more active than usual in the early afternoon. Casualties 5. O.R. wounded	
	6		Cleaning up and refitting; enemy shelled AVELUY intermittently	
	7		A + B Coys stood by awaiting orders to go back to the line; C + D Coys Lewis Gunners and Signallers improved tops in the afternoon. AVELUY again shelled intermittently	
	8		C and D Coys relieved 2 Coys of Devon Fusiliers in front and 2nd line N.E. of THIEPVAL. C in front line, D in second line: relief complete 7 pm. BHs HR at R 26.b. 5.7. A Coy relieved C Coy and B Coy relieved D Coy in reserve near MOUQUET FARM. Major BOLTON in command of C+D Coys; C.O. remained at AVELUY. 1 O.R killed	

Army Form C. 2118.

WAR DIARY
or
INTELLIGENCE SUMMARY

(Erase heading not required.)

Instructions regarding War Diaries and Intelligence Summaries are contained in F. S. Regs., Part II. and the Staff Manual respectively. Title Pages will be prepared in manuscript.

Place	Date	Hour	Summary of Events and Information	Remarks and references to Appendices
	Dec 9th		Intermittent shelling of Posts and STUFF Trench; very wet. Bn H.Q. moved at 2 p.m. to huts operated by Pte Warwicks at W.10.C. A & B Coys relieved 12 noon by 2 Coys 6th Warwicks. C & D Coys relieved 8 p.m. by other two Coys same Battalion. Coys on relief marched to huts at W.10.C.	
	10.			
	11.		225 men working party on PIONEER ROAD 9th; remainder resting and cleaning up.	
	12.		Bn marched to HEDAUVILLE and went into huts. Order of march A. B. C. D. H.Q. Bn started 9.25 a.m.; billeting complete 1 p.m. Snow in early morning changing to rain; very wet and counting of camp very bad.	
	13.		Cleaning up; baths at SENLIS; 2nd Lt TUPMAN went on leave.	
	14.		Training.	
	15.		Training and work on improvement of huts.	
	16.		ditto - ditto -	
	17.		Church parade for 1 platoon per Coy; inspection of huts by C.O.	
	18.		Training; clothes and blankets disinfected in Thresh disinfector.	

2449 Wt. W14957/M90 750,000 1/16 J.B.C. & A. Forms/C.2118/12.

Army Form C. 2118.

WAR DIARY
or
INTELLIGENCE SUMMARY
(Erase heading not required.)

Instructions regarding War Diaries and Intelligence Summaries are contained in F. S. Regs., Part II. and the Staff Manual respectively. Title Pages will be prepared in manuscript.

Place	Date	Hour	Summary of Events and Information	Remarks and references to Appendices
	19th Dec		C. Coy Training; D Coy working party under Div Bombing Officer. A & B Coys employed in improving camp.	
	20		C. Coy and 1 pl. D. Coy working party under 9th Labour Bn on NORTHUMBERLAND AVENUE. Remainder of Bn road surveying and improving camp.	
	21		B Coy and 1 pl A Coy repairing road NORTHUMBERLAND AVENUE. C Coy Training remainder of Bn improving camp.	
	22		Bn marched to AVELUY and relieved 2/6 WARWICKS in huts at W.10.c. Start 9 a.m. Order of march A.B, 2 pl C. Remainder of B's working party at PIONEER ROAD S.E. Billeting complete 11.30 a.m. Work started in afternoon improving camp. Very wet day	
	23		A.B.D. 2 pl C. working party under 1/5 D.L.L.I. at W.10. d.4.4. Remainder of Bn improving camp.	
	24		A. C.D. and 2 pl A Coys working parties, under 1/5 D.L.L.I.	
	25		B & 1 pl. D. working party under 2 field Coy at X.2.a.3.2. A. Coy and 1 pl. C. working on roads.	
	26		A. Coy; 3 pl. C. Coy, 2 pl D Coy working party under 2/ field Coy; 2 pl. D Coy and 1 pl. C Coy carrying platoons at PIONEER ROAD S.E. B Coy on communication trenches	
	27		A Coy, C Coy, 1 pl D Coy working party X.2.a.3.2. - Cable trenging - B Coy working on communication trenches. D Coy carrying platoons at PIONEER ROAD S.E.	

Army Form C. 2118.

WAR DIARY
or
INTELLIGENCE SUMMARY
(Erase heading not required.)

Instructions regarding War Diaries and Intelligence Summaries are contained in F. S. Regs., Part II. and the Staff Manual respectively. Title Pages will be prepared in manuscript.

Place	Date	Hour	Summary of Events and Information	Remarks and references to Appendices
	Dec 28		D Coy, 'C Coy and 1 pl. B Coy working party at AVELUY SIDING. A Coy returned 1 Coy 2/4 Berks at R 26 a and R 2 6. b and became work company in close support. Relief complete 8.30 p.m. Remainder of Bn went into WELLINGTON HUTS relieving 2/5th Gloucesters: relief complete 12 noon; working parties taken in the afternoon.	
	29		B, C, & D Coys working parties in the afternoon at Rifle Dump and Gravel Pit.	
	30		B,C & D Coys working parties at ZOLLERN and HESSIAN and O.P.'s. B Coy moved into dug-outs near Cole St. To make room for a Coy of 2/5 Warwicks.	
	31		B, C & D Coys C Coy brought WARWICK HUTS to make room for a Coy H 2/8 Warwicks. Working parties reporting at RIFLE DUMP and GRAVEL PIT for work in FABECK IZELERN and HESSIAN dugouts; laying duck-boards and digging down near TULLOCHS CORNER.	

S.J. Stutsbury
Capt. &OC
2/4th Bn. Gloucester R.

Vol 9

G.9

CONFIDENTIAL.

WAR DIARY.

of the

2nd 4th. BN. the GLOUCESTERSHIRE REGIMENT.

VOL. 9

JANUARY 1917.

# WAR DIARY / INTELLIGENCE SUMMARY
2/4th Bn - Glos: Regt:
Army Form C. 2118.

Place	Date	Hour	Summary of Events and Information	Remarks and references to Appendices
	1917 Jan 1st		2/4 Glosters relieved 2/6 Glosters in Left Subsection: BHQ at ZOLLERN REDOUBT. 2/6 Glosters relieved A Coy 2/6 Glosters. Relief was complete at 9.50 p.m. and successfully carried out without casualties. The enemy was unusually quiet and it was afterwards ascertained from prisoners that he was carrying out a relief himself. C " " " " B " " " " A " " " "	
	2nd		Enemy artillery active during the day especially on FIELD and HESSIAN trenches and at the junction of these trenches. REGINA and DESIRE trenches were also shelled. Things were quiet. A prisoner was taken in the morning by one of our patrols. He was a Lance Corporal of the 7th Coy FUSILIER REGT	
	3rd		Enemy shelling not as heavy as previous day but a certain number fell in FIELD and HESSIAN trenches, especially at the junction. REGINA and DESIRE trenches and BAINBRIDGE POST were also shelled and during the night STUMP ROAD was heavily bombarded. There was also a good deal of hostile shelling in our back areas. Three prisoners of the 86th FUSILIER REGT were captured at 5.15 p.m. at R.15.d.5. One was a Corporal	
	4th		STUMP ROAD, REGINA Trench, SIXTEENTH ST, HESSIAN Trench and BAINBRIDGE POST shelled intermittently; shelling was less heavy than usual. Relief orders received	

WAR DIARY

INTELLIGENCE SUMMARY

Army Form C. 2118.

(Erase heading not required.)

Place	Date	Hour	Summary of Events and Information	Remarks and references to Appendices
	Jan 5th		Fine bright day and much aerial activity. Less artillery fire than usual. ZOLLERN REDOUBT was twice shelled with 5.9's. DESIRE THIESSEN Trenches and BAINBRIDGE POST were also shelled during the day. A good deal of wire was put out at night. No wire there every night up the line; junction was effected with B's on our right but on our left there was still a gap in the wire when we relieved. 1 O.R. wounded.	
	Jan 6th		Intense bombardment by our guns for 10 minutes starting at 12 noon; enemy retaliated between 2 and 3 p.m. on BAINBRIDGE POST and on DESIRE REGINA, FIELD & HESSIAN Trenches especially at junction of two & not manned, a place which invariably received the heaviest shelling. 2/4 Glosters relieved by 2/5 Warwicks, relief complete 9.10 p.m. A Coy 2/5 Warwicks relieved D Coy 2/4 Glosters. C " " C " B " " A " D " " B " Relief was successfully carried out, the enemy being exceptionally quiet. Bn marched to huts at W.q.d. 1 O.R. wounded.	
	Jan 7th		Cleaning up and resting. C.O. went on leave.	

Army Form C. 2118.

WAR DIARY
INTELLIGENCE SUMMARY
(Erase heading not required.)

Instructions regarding War Diaries and Intelligence Summaries are contained in F. S. Regs., Part II. and the Staff Manual respectively. Title Pages will be prepared in manuscript.

Place	Date	Hour	Summary of Events and Information	Remarks and references to Appendices
	Jan 8th		Bn marched to THEDAUVILLE and took over huts occupied by 2/4 Oxfords. Route NORTHUMBERLAND AVENUE — BOUZINCOURT. Started 9.40 am. Billeting complete 12.15 pm. Fine day. Capt G.D. BARNSLEY rejoined Bn after 3 months absence in a course in England and took over command during C.O.'s absence on leave.	
"	9th		cleaning up. baths	
	10th		Training	
	11th		Training. disinfection of blankets	
	12th		Training. baths	
	13th		Training	
	14th		Church Parade: C.O.'s inspection of Bn.	
	15th		Repitting of toys and cleaning up. 1 Officer reinforcement 2/Lt Q. RIFFIN E.W.	
	16th		Bn marched to RAINCHEVAL (7 miles) and VARENNES – LEAUVILLERS – ARQUEVES. Start 8.55 am. Billeting complete 1 pm. Fine frosty day.	
	17th		Bn marched to AUTHEUX via BEAUQUESNES — Fare du ROSEL – CANDAS – FIENVILLERS. Start 9.52 am. (13½ miles) Snow made roads very bad and slippery. Mules not ready all day. Cookers could not keep up pro that no dinners could be obtained on the way. Billeting complete 5 pm.	
	18th		Bn marched to BEAUMETZ, and to BERNAVILLE. Billeting complete 5 pm. Snow	

WAR DIARY or INTELLIGENCE SUMMARY

Army Form C. 2118.

Instructions regarding War Diaries and Intelligence Summaries are contained in F.S. Regs., Part II. and the Staff Manual respectively. Title Pages will be prepared in manuscript.

(Erase heading not required.)

Place	Date	Hour	Summary of Events and Information	Remarks and references to Appendices
	Jan 19		Bn marched to ARGENVILLERS - via DOMLEGER - YVRENCH - GAPENNES - billetting complete 1 p.m. Fine cold day.	
	20		Cleaning up and resting. C.O. returned from leave	
	21		"	
	22		" 1 officer reinforcement arrived 2/Lt RAGGETT E.L.	
	23		Section and platoon training. Cold fine weather	
	24		" " 4 officer reinforcements	2/Lt BUNN R.W.E. VAUGHAN M.F. CLEAVER T.A. FLEMMING S.H.
	25		22 O.R. Reinforcements	
			Section and platoon training. Lieut Hand-Formed and new cast of Instruments received. Promotion of Capt D.G. BARNSLEY to temp'y Major and his appointment to 2ic in Command, also appointment of Capt S.J. STOTESBURY as adjutant - appeared by Corps Commander. Fine cold weather	
	26		Section and platoon training. Heather colder and much last wind	
	27		"	
	28		Church Parade	
	29		Range practice in the attack inspection of Battn by Corps Commander	
	30		"	
	31		Range practice in the attack	

G.W. Walton Lt Col
Comdg 2/6 Glosters

Vol 10

CONFIDENTIAL

WAR DIARY
of the
2/4th Bn. Gloucestershire Regiment
VOL. 10.

Army Form C. 2118.

WAR DIARY
or
INTELLIGENCE SUMMARY.
(Erase heading not required.)

Instructions regarding War Diaries and Intelligence Summaries are contained in F. S. Regs., Part II. and the Staff Manual respectively. Title pages will be prepared in manuscript.

Place	Date	Hour	Summary of Events and Information	Remarks and references to Appendices
	Feb. 1st		Training: warning order for move from ARGENVILLERS received	
	2nd		Battalion in "attack practice"	
	3rd		Training	
	4th		Battalion marched to FAMECHON — route ST RIQUIER — AILLY-LE-HAUT-CLOCHER. Start 9.5 am — billeting complete 1.30 pm. Fine cold day	
	5th		Training	
	6th		Training — C.O.'s inspection	
	7th		Training	
	8th		G.O.C. Division inspected the Battalion carrying out the attack practice	
	9th		Training	
	10th		Training	
	11th		Church Parade	
	12th		Transport started on 3 days march to new area — 1st day FAMECHON to ST SAVOUR — 2nd day ST SAVOUR to AUBIGNY — 3rd day	

Army Form C. 2118.

WAR DIARY
or
INTELLIGENCE SUMMARY.
(Erase heading not required.)

Instructions regarding War Diaries and Intelligence Summaries are contained in F. S. Regs., Part II. and the Staff Manual respectively. Title pages will be prepared in manuscript.

Place	Date	Hour	Summary of Events and Information	Remarks and references to Appendices
	12th		AUBIGNY & B Staging area. Detailed orders were issued by Brigade. Transport officer on the march.	
	13th 14th		Training	
			Bn marched to PONT REMY STN – route AILLY-LE-HAUT CLOCHER. Start 12.10 pm; arrived station 2.45 pm; train due at 4 pm arrived at 7.15 pm. Entrainment was carried out in 20 minutes. Train left at 7.50 pm and arrived at MARCELCAVE at 12.30 am. Bn marched to WIENCOURT arriving about 2 am 16th	
	15th		C.O. Adjt. and Company Commanders reconnoitred trenches to be taken over from the French.	
	16th		Bn marched to FRAMERVILLE; route GUILLAUCOURT – HARBONNIÈRES – VAUVILLERS. Start 2.30 pm; trekking complete 6 pm. 1 officer per Coy, 1 N.C.O. per Platoon. Signallers & gun gunners were sent to trenches in motor lorries.	
	17th	10.45 pm	Relieved 1st Bn 104th Regiment in PRESSOIRE sector; relief complete 10.45 pm. Route RAINCOURT – HERLEVILLE – VERMANDOVILLERS.	

A5834 Wt.W4973/M687 750,000 8/16 D. D. & L. Ltd. Forms/C.2118/13.

Army Form C. 2118.

WAR DIARY
or
INTELLIGENCE SUMMARY.
(Erase heading not required.)

Instructions regarding War Diaries and Intelligence Summaries are contained in F. S. Regs., Part II. and the Staff Manual respectively. Title pages will be prepared in manuscript.

Place	Date	Hour	Summary of Events and Information	Remarks and references to Appendices
	17th Sept (?)		C Coy 2/4 Glosters relieved a French Company in P.2. (left)	
			B - - - - - P.1. (right)	
			A - - - - - support	
			D - - - - - reserve at VERMANDOVILLERS and BOIS KALVER	
			B² HQ at ROUSSKY, B² frontage S.24.d.7.8 – S.24.c.7.0. (VERMANDOVILLERS 10,000) The relief was accomplished without incident; front line and support Companies entering by SERPENTIN trench. Effect of thaw was already noticeable on the trenches which were not revetted. The French left behind one officer and 3 O.R. per Company also 2 officers at Bn HR. These remained until Sept. 19th/20th.	
	18th		Thaw continued and waters rose rapidly in the trenches, becoming a trouble in many places by the evening. Quiet day except for a few aerial torpedoes on left front (by French 75's) gave immediate retaliation. 1 O.R. killed	
	19th		Quiet day: front extended to S.30.a.3.8. 1 Company-frontage held by 2/7 Worcestors being taken over. A Company moved 1 platoon from VERDUN to ROUSSKY and became left support Company. D Company moved up to dug-outs in S.32.b. (Boyan SERPENTIN - Boyan SAXON) and became right support Coy. Bn HQ moved to CHAULNES, S.23.b.9.6. 2nd in command, M.O. Signalling Officer, Lewis Gun officer and Bombing officer remained at VERDUN. Quiet day. Thaw continued and water was now knee-deep in many places making ration-carrying a very difficult problem. 1 O.R. wounded.	

WAR DIARY or INTELLIGENCE SUMMARY.

(Erase heading not required.)

Army Form C. 2118.

Place	Date	Hour	Summary of Events and Information	Remarks and references to Appendices
	Feb 20th		Quiet day; condition of trenches becoming worse	
	21st	2½ am	2/6 Gloster relieved 2/4 Gloster: A Coy 2/4 Gloster relieved by A Coy 2/6 Gloster	
			B " " B	
			C " " C	
			D " " D	
			Relief commenced at 6 p.m. 21st but owing to the very bad state of the C.T. was not complete until 8.50 a.m. 22nd. Trenches were in many places waist deep in mud and water after relief the Bn marched to billets occupied by 2/6 Gloster at FRAMERVILLE and became B⁹ in Brigade Reserve. The time in the trenches was a very trying one owing to the appalling conditions brought about by the thaw after nearly six weeks frost. Two hot meals a day were carried up the C.T. which was 2¼ miles long to the front line companies. On the 21st inst 2/Lt BIRD received a slight wound from a trap-mortar (accidental) but remained at duty. 14 cases of "trench foot" occurred	
	22nd		1 Officer reinforcement 2/Lt JOHNSON joined	
	23rd		Cleaning up and bathing. Kit inspection	
	24th		Training	

Army Form C. 2118.

WAR DIARY
or
INTELLIGENCE SUMMARY.
(Erase heading not required.)

Instructions regarding War Diaries and Intelligence Summaries are contained in F. S. Regs., Part II. and the Staff Manual respectively. Title pages will be prepared in manuscript.

Place	Date	Hour	Summary of Events and Information	Remarks and references to Appendices
	25th		182 Bde relieved in front line by 182 Bde. Battalion marched to GUILLAUCOURT - VAUVILLERS - HARBONNIÈRES. Billeting complete 6.45 p.m.	
	26th		Training	
	27th		Training; 60 men of B Coy on coal fatigue under O.C. Div Supply Column	
	28th		Training 30 men of C Coy on usual fatigue	

J.S. Kennedy Major
7th S/Staff R.
28/2/17

Vol XI 183/161
March 17

Confidential.

War Diary

of the

2/4th Battalion Gloucestershire Regt

Vol. 11.

Army Form C. 2118.

WAR DIARY
or
INTELLIGENCE SUMMARY.
(Erase heading not required.)

Instructions regarding War Diaries and Intelligence Summaries are contained in F. S. Regs., Part II. and the Staff Manual respectively. Title pages will be prepared in manuscript.

Place	Date	Hour	Summary of Events and Information	Remarks and references to Appendices
	MARCH		Bn	
	1		Bn in Reserve : Bn at GUILLAUCOURT : Training	
	2		Training	
	3		Training	
	4		Church Parade	
	5		Training - baths.	
	6		Training - baths	
	7		Bn marched to FRAMERVILLE, arriving 8.30 p.m. O.C. trip reconnoitre trenches	
	8		Bn went into the line, relieving 2 companies of 2/6 Warwick (left and support) and 2 companies 2/8 Warwick (centre and right)	
			B Coy ——— A Coy ——— D Coy	
			(PRESSOIRE) (KRATZ WOOD) (AMBÈRE, Tr)	
			C	
			(MARCHAND)	
			Frontage S 24.d.4.4 — S 29.a.5.7 (nr VERMANDOVILLERS 10000)	
			Relief was accomplished by 11.45 p.m. without incident : enemy quiet : winter frost ; moonlight night	

Army Form C. 2118.

WAR DIARY
of
INTELLIGENCE SUMMARY.
(Erase heading not required.)

Instructions regarding War Diaries and Intelligence Summaries are contained in F. S. Regs., Part II. and the Staff Manual respectively. Title pages will be prepared in manuscript.

Place	Date	Hour	Summary of Events and Information	Remarks and references to Appendices
	9		Enemy prepare active : little hostile artillery : dull day and some rain.	
	10		Heavy bombardment of CHAULNES by our artillery during the afternoon. Fine bright day.	
	11		Artillery registration on both sides. Moderate aerial activity. 2/Lt HADLEY and 1 O.R. wounded. Fine day.	
	12		Enemy active with aerial torpedos chiefly opposite PRESSOIRE. Four officer reinforcements arrives ⎨ 2/Lt Eayley " BAKER " Stanier " Wookey	
	13		Quiet day	
	14/15		2/6 Glosters relieve 2/4 Glosters : owing to the mud and a very dark night the relief which started at 6.30 pm was not complete until 4 am. B Coy 2/4 Glosters relieved A Coy 2/6 Glosters A D C C D B Bn moved back into close support. H.Q. at LYAUTEY : 2 coys (C+D) in VERMANDOVILLERS 1 Coy (B) S.27.a.9.8 : 1 Coy (A) S.21.d.9.0 (just VERMANDOVILLERS)	
	15		2/Lt DUDDLE accidentally wounded.	

Army Form. C. 2118.

WAR DIARY
or
INTELLIGENCE SUMMARY.
(Erase heading not required.)

Instructions regarding War Diaries and Intelligence Summaries are contained in F. S. Regs., Part II. and the Staff Manual respectively. Title pages will be prepared in manuscript.

Place	Date	Hour	Summary of Events and Information	Remarks and references to Appendices
	16th		Working parties	
	17th		Definite information received that enemy had vacated his line; large fires were observed in his back areas. Preparations made for advance the following day.	
	18th		Bn. advanced at 9.30 am and took up a position in old German line in KRATZ Wood. Bn. was left outpost Bn. in Bde.	
	19th		Bn. advanced to POTTE, route HYENCOURT LE GRAND – OMIECOURT – PERTAHN. Houses and dug-outs burnt. Most of the men had to bivouac during the night. Transport lines and Q.M. stores remained at FRAMERVILLE.	
	20th		Work on clearing roads of wire and making new roads around craters blown in roads; craters at:- B.18.a.10.2, B.24.d.3.2, MOLCHAIN. (Ref. 66.d) Accommodation found for all the men in cellars and dug-outs.	
	21st		Work on roads continued.	
	22nd		Bn. took over work of 96 Sqdn. in C 21 & C 27 (Ref. 66.d)	
	23rd		Work on string points in the morning; Bn. moved to CROIX MOLIGNAUX starting 3 pm. arrived 5.30 pm. Village badly damaged; men billeted in cellars. D-Coy. found outpost troops – line MATIGNY – CROIX MOTIGNAUX – S.E. corner of BOIS de CROIX ; 2/8 Warwicks on left and 1st Dorsets on right	

A 5834 Wt. W4973/M687 750,000 8/16 D. D. & L. Ltd. Forms/C.2118/13.

Army Form C. 2118.

WAR DIARY
or
INTELLIGENCE SUMMARY.
(Erase heading not required.)

Instructions regarding War Diaries and Intelligence Summaries are contained in F. S. Regs., Part II. and the Staff Manual respectively. Title pages will be prepared in manuscript.

Place	Date	Hour	Summary of Events and Information	Remarks and references to Appendices
	24:9		Work on strong points and putting village in a state of defence. work on craters.	
	25:9		Work on craters. Coy. pent to COULAINCOURT to come under orders of AMBALA Cavalry Bde. 1 Officer reinforcement arrived. 2/Lt HARRIS.	
	26:9		Work on craters at Southern entrance to MONCHY LAGACHE. Q.M. stores & transport moved to LIHONS from FRAMERVILLE	
	27:9		A, B & D Coys working on craters at Southern entrance MONCHY LAGACHE. Q.M. stores moved from LIHONS to CROIX MOLIGNAUX. B Coy moved to MONCHY LAGACHE, move complete 9.15 p.m. 2.OR. (O.Ey) killed by shell fire at COULAINCOURT	
	28:9		Q.M. stores moved to MONCHY LAGACHE. A Coy moved to COULAINCOURT and became front line Bn in left sub-section - move complete 10 p.m. 78 Wores in support 2/y Warwicks in left. Line of resistance COULAINCOURT with 5 posts thrown out about 200y East of village - enemy holding VERMAND and MARTEVILLE strongly. Intermittent shelling of village by 77's. Village very much damaged by enemy in retreat. Bn. Hq. in cellar at Chateau. Dispositions: A Coy - left front B " " right " C " left support D " right support Weather cold - many ↑↓↓↑	

WAR DIARY
or
INTELLIGENCE SUMMARY.

Army Form C. 2118.

Place	Date	Hour	Summary of Events and Information	Remarks and references to Appendices
	29th		Work in defence of village: men rested.	
	30th		Patrols from A+D Coy sent out at 3.30 am to discover if VERMAND was still occupied. Patrols fired on from cemetery W. of VERMAND and withdrew. 2. O.R. missing. A Coy relieved by 2/5 Gloster & 2/4 R. Berks. Bn. marched to TREFCON and took over billets of 2/5 Worcs. VERMAND occupied during night by 184 Bde without resistance.	
	31st		Work in defence of village. Any sent forward & attached to 2/8 Worcs at VILLEVEQUE 2 coys 2/6 Gloster attached to 2/4 Gloster.	

Lt Col
Comdg 2/4 Glosters

Vol 12

G.12

Confidential

War Diary.

of the

2/4ᵗʰ Battalion, The Gloucestershire Regiment

Vol. 12.

WAR DIARY
INTELLIGENCE SUMMARY.
(Erase heading not required.)

Army Form C. 2118.

Place	Date	Hour	Summary of Events and Information	Remarks and references to Appendices
	April 1st		Work on defences of TREFCON and on craters. Battalion marched at 6pm to VILLEVEQUE and took over outpost line of 2/4 Worcesters. Orders were received at midnight that the Brigade would carry out an attack at 5am the objectives being the MILL at R.28.c.7.5.; Mount HUETTE wood and village of VILLDEHELLES; 184th Brigade attacking North of River OMIGNON (Ref. 62.c.S.E. 2/20000)	
	2nd		Above orders were cancelled at 2am. as objection had already been raised. Further orders were received at 9 am. that the Brigade would attack the line MAISSEMY and Ridge South of MAISSEMY with three Battalions at 3 p.m. — 2/4 Glosters centre — 2/4 Worcesters left — 1/6 Glosters right — 1/8 Worcesters left. Objective of 2/4 Glosters was the ridge from R.30.a.11. to R.23.d.7.5. Information was received at 9.15 a.m. that Cavalry patrols were already in possession of the objective. Bn. moved forward at 10 am. to objective and started consolidation of line. Heavy enemy shelling during the afternoon; fire slackened during the night. A series of posts were dug; A, B + C coys being in the front line and D coy in support. Bn. H.Q. in a shelter about R.23.d.7.0. (Ref. 62.c.S.E. 1/20000) Fine day but blizzard came on during the night –	
	3rd		Battalion withdrawn into support at MARTEVILLE: 2 coys in the village and 2 coys at R.33.d.7.0. (62.c.S.E.) the line was taken over by 1/4 Worces on left and 1/6 Glos. on right. Much "sniping". There were no billets in MARTEVILLE as all houses were blown up from the cellars. Rain and snow	
	4th		Work on roads and craters and improvement of billets.	

WAR DIARY
INTELLIGENCE SUMMARY.
(Erase heading not required.)

Army Form C. 2118.

Place	Date	Hour	Summary of Events and Information	Remarks and references to Appendices
	5th		Work on roads and craters and improvement of trenches. 2 companies sent at 4 pm to 2/6 Glosters. A report to 2/6 Glosters. Raiders report 15/6 Glos; at 6 pm. these companies took over the line to 2/6 Glosters. 2/6 Glosters made an attack on FRESNOY but were held up by M.G. fire.	
	6th		Battalion relieved 2/6 Glosters; orders being received at 2 a.m. Relief was complete at 6 a.m. A line of posts taken up West of FRESNOY 2 companies in support at HOT-NON WOOD which were heavily shelled during the day. Div Artillery bombarded FRESNOY in the afternoon. The Battalion carried out an attack on FRESNOY in conjunction with 2/8 when attacking BETHANCOURT BERTHAUCOURT and hill 120 on our left. D and B Coys advanced at 9.10 p.m. under artillery barrage. Companies were held up in the front of Village by wire in front of trenches and by heavy rifle and M.G. fire. An attempt was made to cut the wire, turning on the artillery again and use of Stokes mortars. This proved ineffectual and a line was therefore consolidated in the Village during the night about 300x from enemy trench location of which was about - M.21 Central - M.27 to 3.9. - M.27.9.4. 262.13 approx Snow and sleet. Casualties 10 O.R. killed - 13 O.R. wounded.	
	7th		Quiet day - relieved by 2/4 Warwicks; relief complete 10.55 p.m. Bt. marched to TREFCON. Very cold day - snow. 1 OR killed - 1 OR missing.	
	8th		Clearing up - fine sunny day	
	9th		Working parties on roads and craters in the morning. At 3 pm Bt. marched to	

Army Form C. 2118.

WAR DIARY
— or —
INTELLIGENCE SUMMARY.
(Erase heading not required.)

Instructions regarding War Diaries and Intelligence Summaries are contained in F. S. Regs., Part II. and the Staff Manual respectively. Title pages will be prepared in manuscript.

Place	Date	Hour	Summary of Events and Information	Remarks and references to Appendices
	April 9th	9am	FIEZ and DOUVIEUX. Bn H.Q., B₁ 2 Coys at FIEZ. A & D Coys Q.M. Stores and Transport lines at DOUVIEUX, cold showery day	
	10th		Working parties on roads and craters – snow	
	11th		ditto – rain	
	12th		ditto – ditto	
	13th		A & D Coys working on roads. C.O. inspected C & B Coys in morning. Drenching fine day.	
	14th		C & D Coys working on roads. C.O. inspected A & D Coys in morning. B₂ parade in afternoon. Rain.	
	15th		A & B Coys working on roads – C & D Coys training. rain.	
	16th		Work on roads. Rain	
	17th		ditto ditto	
	18th		Work of defensive line – COULAINCOURT – TREFCON rain	
	19th		ditto ditto	
	20th		ditto fine day	

Army Form C. 2118.

WAR DIARY
or
INTELLIGENCE SUMMARY.
(Erase heading not required.)

Instructions regarding War Diaries and Intelligence Summaries are contained in F. S. Regs., Part II. and the Staff Manual respectively. Title pages will be prepared in manuscript.

Place	Date	Hour	Summary of Events and Information	Remarks and references to Appendices
	April 21st		Work on road GUIZANCOURT - MONCHY LAGACHE. As marched to GERMAINE - HENIN - QUIVIERES - UGNY - FORESTE. As billeted in one large farm. Fine day. Military cross awarded to 200737 Pte HAWKINS; 235001 Cpl FOWLER; 201847 Cpl FLEMMING for gallantry at night 6th & 7th April	
	22nd		Work on cleaning up billets and surroundings. Fine day.	
	23rd		2 hrs training - remainder of day cleaning up billets.	
	24th		2 trips working in VAUX craters: remainder working in billets & huts	
	25th		Baths	
	26th		Training	
	27th		Training	
	28th		Working parties VAUX; EREILLERS & SAVY. C.O. went on leave. Major BARNSLEY in command.	
	29th		Church Parade. 2/Lt. SHIPWAY awarded M.C. for gallantry on night 6th/7th April	
	30th		Training	
			Strength - Casualties - reinforcements are appendix A.	B Barnsley Major 2/4 Lt Yorks LI Comdg 2/4 Lt Yorks LI

1st Bn Gloucestershire Regt

Appendix A to War Diary.

	Date	Officers	OR	Date	Officers	OR	Remarks
Effective Strength	1-4-17	43	742	30-4-17	43	736	-
Ration Strength	1-4-17	35	615	30-4-17	30	616	-

Explanation of Reinforcements & Casualties.

Reinforcements during April — 30 OR.

Casualties:-
 Evacuated Sick   OR
          10
 " Wounded   14
 Commissions   2
 Transfers   6
 To Base for Dental Treatment 1
 Killed in Action   3
 Missing   —
          36

Net Decrease in Strength   16

2/4th Bn Gloucestershire Regt. Vol 13

WAR DIARY.

Volume 13.
May. 1917.

G.13

Army Form C. 2118.

WAR DIARY
or
INTELLIGENCE SUMMARY.
(Erase heading not required.)

Instructions regarding War Diaries and Intelligence Summaries are contained in F. S. Regs., Part II. and the Staff Manual respectively. Title pages will be prepared in manuscript.

Place	Date	Hour	Summary of Events and Information	Remarks and references to Appendices
GERMAINE	May 1st		Writing Parties and Training. Bn. Parade in the afternoon for presentation of decorations by G.O.C. Division.	
	2nd		Bn. relieved the 2/4 Bucks in right Subsect. Headquarters at S.24.7 (Sheet 62c S.W.) C Coy men relieved in MOLHAIN; B & A Coys in Shelters in S.7a. Relief complete by 11.35 p.m.	
	3rd		Work in BROWN LINE completed.	
	4th		do	
	5th		do	
	6th		Work on BROWN LINE completed. Begun new work at S26.33. Support Coy (A Coy in the right) & S26.33. B & Outpost Line & French, ch. right work for Brown Posts. The line ran approximately 200' behind the Outpost Line. A case of attack, Support Battalions would man the BROWN LINE; one Coy being kept in Readiness A; the B Bn. H.Q. in a cellar on HAHAM at ST6.15. (alphine). Force on new defensive line, two Coys working the night in two posts on S26 to form Coys 2 outpost Bn. H.Q.	
	7th		Work on new defensive Line; two new posts dug.	
	8th		Work on new defensive Line.	
	9th		do	
	10th		The 2/4 Gloucesters relieved the 2/4 Berks on the OUTPOST LINE & Coy 2/4 Glos. relieved R Coy 2/4 Worcesters night:—	
			A " " " " B " "	
			B " " " " C " "	
			C " " " " A " "	

WAR DIARY or INTELLIGENCE SUMMARY

Army Form C. 2118.

(Erase heading not required.)

Instructions regarding War Diaries and Intelligence Summaries are contained in F. S. Regs., Part II. and the Staff Manual respectively. Title pages will be prepared in manuscript.

Place	Date	Hour	Summary of Events and Information	Remarks and references to Appendices
	May 10th		1 Coy 1/ 2/6 Glosters attacked in reserve at Bttn. school room in the dugout at S.52.c.27. The Support line crossed Hug Street & Proto movement at my Battalion Unit. Pts to relieve the Bn. were arranged 10h.24 Patrol who reconnoitered trenches in front and was completed at 3.10 a.m. Quiet night. — rain.	
	11th		Bombardment of enemy trenches on Back area and Enemy communication. Hug Street with 2". Stokes gun. Fire walked tp, Enemy Artillery two actions. Fine day.	
	12th		I Coy moved to CDY. FARM at 1.35 a.m. after being relieved. The New bomb in front of the farm was completely cut. Enemy shewed at the trenches E. of the Farm. Enormous.	
	13th		20th wounded.	
	14th		Quiet day. Patrol sent out and CDY. FARM. Trenches 17th reported to Shelf for 5/4 the Glosters were relieved by the 2/6 Battalions. Pts. 139c	
	15th		French Infantry Regiment. "C" Coy. 2/4 Glosters relieved by 1st Coy 1st Bn. 139e Inf. Reg. (right) "A" — — — 2nd Coy 3rd — — — (right centre) "D" — — — 9th Coy 3rd — — — (left centre) "B" — — — 1st — — — (left) "C" — — — 2/6 — — — . — . — . (reserve) Relief completed by 1.35 a.m. without incident. After relief Battalion marched to GERMAINE. Fines.	
			11Coy. 3rd Bn. & 3rd Coy 1st B.	

Army Form C. 2118.

WAR DIARY
or
INTELLIGENCE SUMMARY.
(Erase heading not required.)

Instructions regarding War Diaries and Intelligence Summaries are contained in F. S. Regs., Part II. and the Staff Manual respectively. Title pages will be prepared in manuscript.

Place	Date	Hour	Summary of Events and Information	Remarks and references to Appendices
	16"		Resting and clearing up. Reinforcements join. More to next mov.	
	17"		B. marched to RUOY LE GRAND - rnd FORESTE - DOUILLY - MATIGNY - BUNY.	
	18"		VOYENNES. Starting 5.5am, arriv 11am. B. marched to NESLE. Starting 7.10am. Entrained at Station and train left at 9.10am. Arriving LONGEAU at 11am. Detrained and marched to BERTANGLES, arriving 4.30pm.	
	19"		Resting	
	20"		"	
	21"		B. marched to BEAUVAL - rnd VILLERS - BOCAGE - TALMAS. Starting 7.10am. and arriv in billets at 11.30am.	
	22"		Resting	
	23"		B. marched to SUS ST. LEGER - rnd DOULLENS - LUNEUX. Starting 6.30am. and arriv in billets 12.30pm	
	24"		B. moved by road out here to DAINVILLE - rnd SOMBRIN - SAULTY. LATBRET - LE BAC du SUD - BERUMETZ. Marched as far as LE BAC du SUD. arr went in huts. Road journey. Arriv't in billets 3.31pm.	
	25"		Clearing up and resting.	
	26"		Training.	
	27"		Training and baths. Cheval parade.	
	28"		Training	
	29"		Training	

Army Form C. 2118.

WAR DIARY
or
INTELLIGENCE SUMMARY.
(Erase heading not required.)

Instructions regarding War Diaries and Intelligence Summaries are contained in F. S. Regs., Part II. and the Staff Manual respectively. Title pages will be prepared in manuscript.

Place	Date	Hour	Summary of Events and Information	Remarks and references to Appendices
Ypres, France	May 31st		Strength, Casualties & Reinforcements. See Appendix B. Special Return in General Muster Form May 13th. See Appendix A.	

R.G. Boulton Lt. Col.
Comdt. 2/4 Glos. Regt.

2/4 Bn Gloucestershire Regiment.

Appendix "D" to War Diary   May 1917.

	Date	Officers	O.R.	Date	Officers	O.R.	Remarks
Effective Strength	May 1st 1917	43	736	May 31st 1917	45	733	net decrease 3.
Ration Strength	May 1st 1917	30	616	May 31st 1917	31	608	

Explanation of Reinforcements and Casualties

Reinforcements received
      Offrs OR
              - 36

Casualties:-
               Offrs OR
  Wounded Evac.   3
  Evacuated Sick.   1 34
  Commission   1
  Transferred A.O.C.   1
                         1 39.

Net Decrease in Strength 1 officer
                                      3. OR

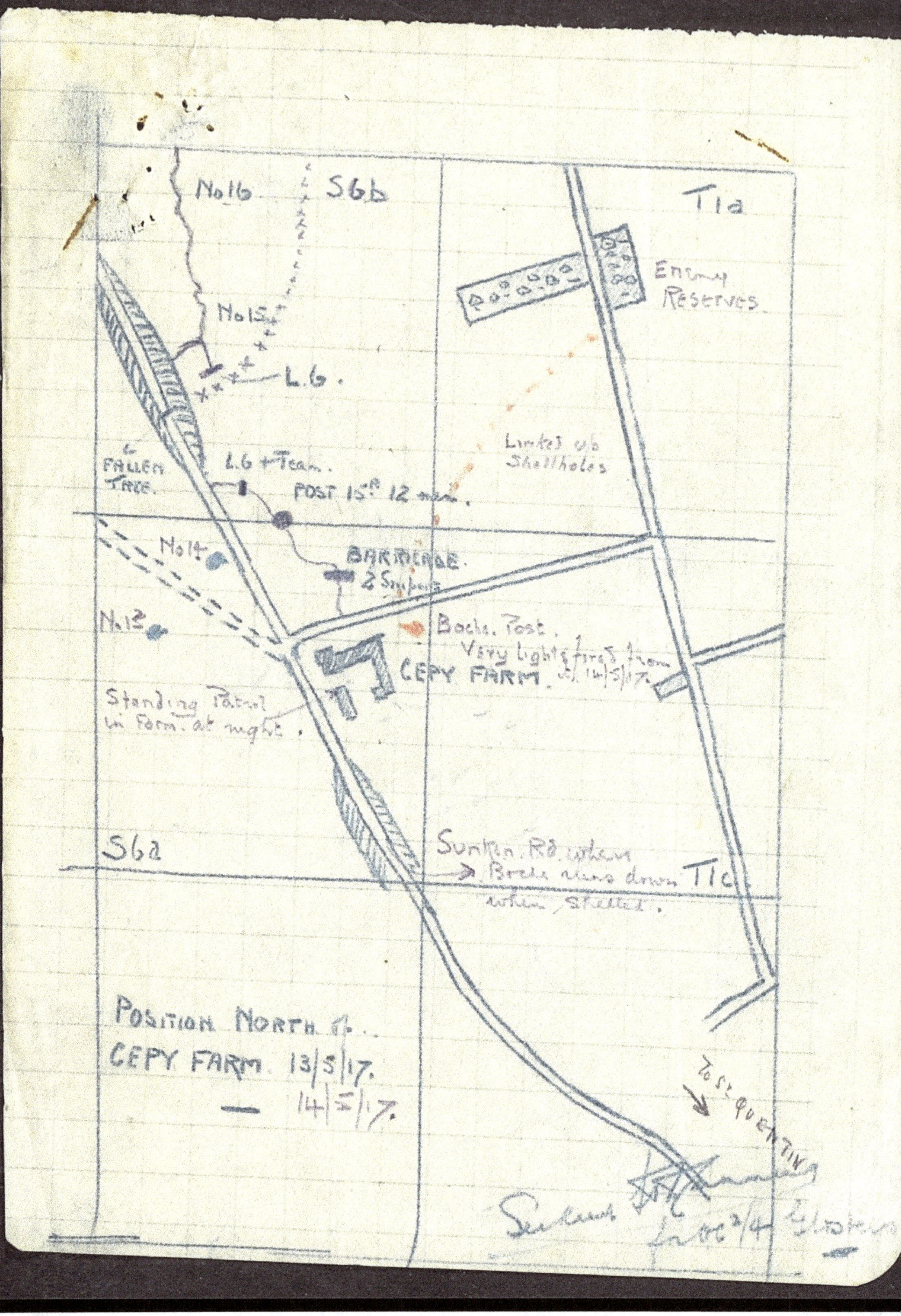

Hand-drawn sketch map on graph paper

Grid squares labelled: **S6b**, **T1a**, **S6a**, **T1c**

- No 16
- No 15
- L.G.
- Fallen Tree
- L.G. + Team. POST 15th 12 men.
- No 14
- BARRICADE & Snipers
- No 13
- Boche Post. Very lights fired from on 14/5/17.
- CEPY FARM
- Standing Patrol in Farm at night.
- Enemy Reserves
- Linked u/b Shellholes
- Sunken Rd where Boche runs down when shelled.
- To St Quentin →

POSITION NORTH of
CEPY FARM. 13/5/17.
— 14/5/17.

Signed from OC 2/4 Glosters

Report —

The arrangements and time-tables worked throughly well. The relief of the Coy. was completed by Coy 2/7 Worcs at 10.50 pm. The Coy. was assembled at Coy HQ, given their hot evening meal from the food containers, organised in their respective parties and armed in accordance with requirements by 12.15 am. They were then led into position and started off by 12.40 am. The raid from this time onwards took place in accordance with schedule. The rousing party, consisting of two Bombing parties and one destruction party rushed the ruins behind the barrage and found the front enemy trenches at 56d 7.5 & 7.5.4 smashed in by the barrage. They searched all the ruins, threw bombs in any corner or recess where the enemy might have been and absolutely cleared the farm. The covering party was up against the trench at S6d 0.2 and were just in time to see about 8 Huns fleeing down the Sunken Road in the direction of the old Mill. Silhouetted against the fires in St Quentin. They fired on these men and claim one hit. The whole party withdrew at the appointed time on discharge of the Signal by the O.C. Raiding Party + at 1.50 am the parties were back at CHQ. All agreed that the arrangements had worked well and that the barrage was admirable, no shells falling short at all. At 2.30 am a patrol consisting of Sub. Griffin who had already led the Raiding party was sent out to pregn the Farm buildings and to prevent the enemy returning to occupy the ground we had driven him out of. They found that the Boche had not returned and settled themselves in the sunken road W of the ruins. At 3.45 am the enemy began a counter-attack. They put a barrage down on the farm & then lifted to the posts at S6d 1.44. No 12. They also bombed our Standing Patrol, but these withdrew owing to the light only, at 4.30 am. In the meantime the remainder of the Coy had relieved the Coy of 2/7 Worcs who eventually got away just before dawn in spite of the enemy shell fire on Hole Post & surroundings.

The three objects of the raid were thus carried out as

The enemy was ejected from the farm ruins, his defences were destroyed and posts were established in the farm who did not withdraw until dawn in spite of the enemy fire. Casualties nil

Sgt. H Chaney
2/4 Glosters

"Cleaver"

According to orders, I took down a Lewis Gun which was in forward post by fallen tree. & established it in trench about 20" right of Roman Rd. where it can fire into copse Farm, & cover the road. Further along this same trench, about 100" a block was made with wire, and a bombing post with a Sniper was posted

2/4th Batt. Gloucestershire Regiment. Vol 14

WAR DIARY.

— Volume 14. —

— June 1917. —

Confidential

WAR DIARY
or
INTELLIGENCE SUMMARY.
(Erase heading not required.)

Army Form C. 2118.

Place	Date	Hour	Summary of Events and Information	Remarks and references to Appendices
Dainville	June 1st		Dainville. Warlus Rd. Shelled by 14" long range gun with artillery observation between 7am & 10am. - Ammunition dumps set on fire. The Bn. relieved the 7th Gordons in The Harp, Tilloy in nights 1st/2nd. - The 173 Inf. Bde. being in Supports. Pnd. Bde. Amiens - Schramm Barracks - Arras Station - Tilloy. Relief complete without incident at 10.15 pm.	
	2nd		Raining much. Never a bright day. Being Jane and Stokes mortar. Hostile artillery active on Bn. Area. and Parene Positions. Baths. Church Parade in the evening	
	3rd			
	4th		Raining and bombardment of Shelters. Hostile Shelling active. Arras Trench at 10.15 bnd	
	5th		Raining. Fine day. Enemy trench mortars from our trenches in the evening. Scarpe Valley shows acute activity in the evening. T.M.s from hostile aeroplane thrown down on Trench. A fight between the Bde. Elect. Huns seen as a result. Heaps of Bait & Ry flying Slones at 7.30 pm. a Bdn. slang trying bars with a fight & amongst the huns. Rain in the night. Bn. to Billets: Henin Field: Vanester appno 10 pm from Henin Artillery L.G. During the night B/1633 to Dainville from Dainville to Support Line.	
	6th		Artillery active during the night on C.T. Morning Gas green lime in Support Line - during in front anea active.	

Army Form C. 2118.

WAR DIARY
or
INTELLIGENCE SUMMARY.
(Erase heading not required.)

Instructions regarding War Diaries and Intelligence Summaries are contained in F. S. Regs., Part II. and the Staff Manual respectively. Title pages will be prepared in manuscript.

Place	Date	Hour	Summary of Events and Information	Remarks and references to Appendices
	7"		Quiet and fine day. Working parties at night.	
	8"		Normal working parties at night	
	9"		do.	
	10"		Quiet day. Bn. arms back to Simencourt at night starting at 9.20 pm. Reg. Arras Station. - Sebroom Barracks - Fbe. Ambers. Berneville. Heavy rain during latter part of march. Feet and cleaning up.	
	11"		Training	
	12"		do.	
	13"		do.	
	14"		do.	
	15"		do. Battalion Sports	
	16"		do.	
	17"		Church Parade. Brigade Sports	
	18"		Training	
	19"		do. Bde Sports	
	20"		Preparations for move. Transport started on a two days march to new area.	
	21"		Bn. marched to Gouy-en-Artois and entrained for Hesdin. Train left at 10.15 am and arrived at Hesdin 3.15 pm. Battalion detrained and marched to Fillievres. nr. St. Austreberthe. St. Georges. Billeting completed 7.15 pm. Showery day.	

Army Form C. 2118.

WAR DIARY
or
INTELLIGENCE SUMMARY.
(Erase heading not required.)

Instructions regarding War Diaries and Intelligence Summaries are contained in F. S. Regs., Part II. and the Staff Manual respectively. Title pages will be prepared in manuscript.

Place	Date	Hour	Summary of Events and Information	Remarks and references to Appendices
	23"		Training	
	24"		Church Parade	
	25"		Training - Bn/S.D. 19th anniv	
	26"		Training	
	27"		Do	
	28"		Do	
	29"		Bde. Horse Show	
	30"			

J.S. Hannahy Major
Cmdr. 7/c ? Bn.
30/6/17.

9th Bn Gloucestershire Regiment

Appendix "A" to War Diary

STRENGTH.	DATE	OFFS	O.R	DATE	OFFS	O.R.
Effective Strength	June 1st 1917	42	723	June 30. 1917.	38	710
Ration Strength	"	24	608	"	23	634

Net Decrease 4 Officers   Net Decrease 13 O.R.

	Off	O.R	Off	O.R.
Reinforcements received:-				
Joined			1	19
Rejoined			1	9
				38
Casualties:-				
Evacuated sick	1	15		
" Wounded		2		
Classified "P.U."		1		
To Base. D.T.		5		
Transferred:-				
IV Corps Schools	3	2		
7th (Sny) Field Co. R.E.		8		
Roads Construction Co		4		
183 T.M.B.		1		
Traffic Control		-		
To England Commission	1			
Retained in England			5	41
			4	13

NET DECREASE:-

2/4th Batt'n Gloucestershire Regt.

Vol 15

WAR DIARY.

VOLUME 15

JULY. 1917.

q.15

Army Form C. 2118.

WAR DIARY
or
INTELLIGENCE SUMMARY.
(Erase heading not required.)

Instructions regarding War Diaries and Intelligence Summaries are contained in F. S. Regs., Part II. and the Staff Manual respectively. Title pages will be prepared in manuscript.

Place	Date	Hour	Summary of Events and Information	Remarks and references to Appendices
Filièvres	July 1st		Church Parade	
	2nd		Training	
	3rd		do	
	4th		do	
	5th		do	
	6th		Final Platoon Embarkation	
	7th		Final Brigade 6th Infantry Embarkation – B Coy winning	
	8th		do	
	9th		do	
	10th		do	
	11th		do	
	12th		do	
	13th		do	
	14th		do	
	15th		Church Parade Bayo	
	16th		Training. Bn Troops to Heroes Attacks Practice	
	17th		do	
	18th		do Inter Coy Race Meeting	
	19th		do	
	20th		do	
	21st		do	
	22nd		Church Parade	
	23rd		Training	
	24th		Battalion moves to NUNCQ ; route. CONCHY – BOUBERS – LIGNY– SUR– CONCHE ; arrived 12 noon.	
	25th		Resting	

Army Form C. 2118.

WAR DIARY
or
INTELLIGENCE SUMMARY.
(Erase heading not required.)

Instructions regarding War Diaries and Intelligence Summaries are contained in F. S. Regs., Part II. and the Staff Manual respectively. Title pages will be prepared in manuscript.

Place	Date	Hour	Summary of Events and Information	Remarks and references to Appendices
	26ᵗʰ		Battalion marched to PETIT-HOUVIN. Scarpe and entrained. Train leaves at following time. B Coy 1.40 a.m. remainder of Battalion 5.19 a.m. Arrived at ESQUELBECQ station. Men marched to HOLLAND. NIEUWLAND area, arriving in hijacks at 5 p.m.	
	27ᵗʰ		Raining.	
	28ᵗʰ		Raining. Wet day. Coys of B.H. and 2ᵗʰ 17ᵗʰ Divisions.	
	29ᵗʰ		Raining.	
	30ᵗʰ			
	31ˢᵗ		B. French attack Service.	

R. Maunter Lt Col

2/4th Batt. Gloucestershire Regiment.

APPENDIX "A" TO WAR DIARY.

Strength.	Date.	Offs.	O.Ranks.	Date.	Offs.	O.R.
Effective Strength.	July 1st.	38	710	July 31st.	39	964.
Ration Strength.	July 1st.	23	634	July 31st.	30	894.

REINFORCEMENTS RECEIVED.   Officers.   Other Ranks.

                            Joined   5   290.
                            Rejoined ...   7.
                                                  _____   _____
                            Total Increase   5   297.

CASUALTIES.

                    To Senior Officers Course.   1   1
                    Joined Royal Flying Corps.   3
                    Trans. to 183 L.T.M.B.   2
                       "   183 Bde.   5
                       "   251 Emp. Coy.   11
                    Attached 251 Emp. Coy.   2.
                    Evacuated sick.   16
                    To Base P.B.   3
                    To Divnl. Gas School.   1.
                    To Headquarters Transportation   1
                                                  _____   _____
                            Total Decrease   4   43

                            NET INCREASE   1   254

183/61.

Vol 16

2/4th Bn. Gloucestershire Regt.

WAR DIARY.

G.16

VOLUME 16.

August 1917.

WAR DIARY or INTELLIGENCE SUMMARY

Army Form C. 2118.

Place	Date	Hour	Summary of Events and Information	Remarks and references to Appendices
Nieuland	Aug 1st		Training	
	2nd		do	
	3rd		do	
	4th		do	
	5th		Church Parade	
	6th		Training	
	7th		Bn. Practice Trench Attack	
	8th		Training	
	9th		do	
	10th		do	
	11th		do	
	12th		Church Parade	
	13th		Training	
	14th		do	
	15th		Bn. marched to ESQUELBECQ. where it entrained at 3 a.m. arriving at HOPOUTRE at 6.30 a.m. and marched to camp no. 81 a O.1. R. 25 N.W. arriving at 7.30 a.m.	
	16th		Bn. arrived here at 6.30 a.m. to YPRES. Much enemy shelling of Ypres, hotter Kemm. Ridge and Kypress were shelled. 36th 9th Regt. Kemm. Artillery fire and great aerial activity all day.	

WAR DIARY
or
INTELLIGENCE SUMMARY

Army Form C. 2118.

Place	Date	Hour	Summary of Events and Information	Remarks and references to Appendices
	2nd		Bn. relieved 8th Royal Scots Regiment in the left subsector WEILTJE. Relief being completed at 4.30 am. Dispositions: D Coy. left front; C Coy. Right front; B Coy. in Support; A Coy. in reserve. Bn. H.Q. at C.9.11 R.m.; Bn. HQ. reserve & forward systems not in the left and 3½ KNOWN to the north.	
	17th		Heavy shelling and aircraft most all day.	
	19th		In conjunction with the 25th Div., much artillery activity. Heavy shelling enemy lines POND FM GRIFRIAS. B Bn. attacked from Km.4.50 am. The Bn. met with heavy trench fire and severe resistance from enemy. Interlacement as C.16.50.0 - Ft. FRIEZENBERG Sheet 1:10,000. Report received that reported on the enemy to Km L.9. and enemy Mach. Guns preventing advancing 3 Km. Diamond Line. DIDDIE who had led by a Lieman Officer when wounded. Two platoons for the remainder of the company is enemy hand. Heavy Artillery fire all day. CPPX from Km extended to shelled from 5.9. No damage. Very fine.	

WAR DIARY
or
INTELLIGENCE SUMMARY.
(Erase heading not required.)

Army Form C. 2118.

Place	Date	Hour	Summary of Events and Information	Remarks and references to Appendices
	23rd		Day quiet then round to fully heavy fire & bombs by the enemy on my support line and men front CALFA reports 9.30-10am.	
			Bn was relieved by 2/4 Oxford Bucks and 1 Coy 2/1 Bucks.	
			Offrs went away to report by 9.30 pm 2/Lt. Hort continued to remain on the line	
			1 Man For KILLED : 7 or MISSING : 29 or WOUNDED	
	2nd		After relief Bn moved back to camp at SOLOGH LEFT 27 V YPRES NORTH AREA. A/c 173 Bde. Cleaning the Bivouac.	
			in Support. 152 Bde. in attack. Resting and refitting.	
	22nd		Bn received 2/Lt Glosters in rest. Old Support line hit	
	23rd		at 7.30 pm the 26 Glosters relieved 2/4 Oxfords in the front line. Relief completed by 7 pm Bn to at WELTJE Fm	
			Hav. Elec. Quing while the motor Bn to at WELTJE Fm received a few Kaiserin gas no pieces her men wounded notices were received.	
	24th		That day.	
	25th		Orders to 173 Bde Reserve received	
	26th		Bn moved into position in Brigade to Staff line from the line for form. Enemy aeroplanes very active.	
			(19 ROSSM KEEP	

WAR DIARY
or
INTELLIGENCE SUMMARY.
(Erase heading not required.)

Army Form C. 2118.

Place	Date	Hour	Summary of Events and Information	Remarks and references to Appendices
	26"		P.O.D. FA GALLERIES. C.15.67.10. Further fire in position by 5am. Bn. transferred at CAPRICORN KEEP.	
	27"		153 Bde Attack - See APPENDIX B. Bn. maps appendix B. Bn. moved to Bn. GLOSTERS. to form line and returned to Bn. RESERVE area running down 5am 25".	
	28"		Coll. Res. Area - Resting	
	29"		Bn. relieved 2/6 GLOSTERS. Coy. Front Line, relief there complete by 12.35 a.m. 30 inst. D Coy. Left A Coy Centre B Coy Right. C Coy in Support. Bn.H.Q. CAPRICORN KEEP. Bn. Support. Battn. Keep.	
	30"		Bn. relieved by 2/7. WARWICKS. relief being complete by 11.30 am. Bn. Regiment by motor lorries to BRANDHOEK. Left area on road arriving at 4.15 5am. 31".	
	31"		Resting.	
			Maps + Reports in Special Operations Aug. 27". See APPENDIX B	

R.P. Moulton? Lt Col
Comdt 2/4 Glosters

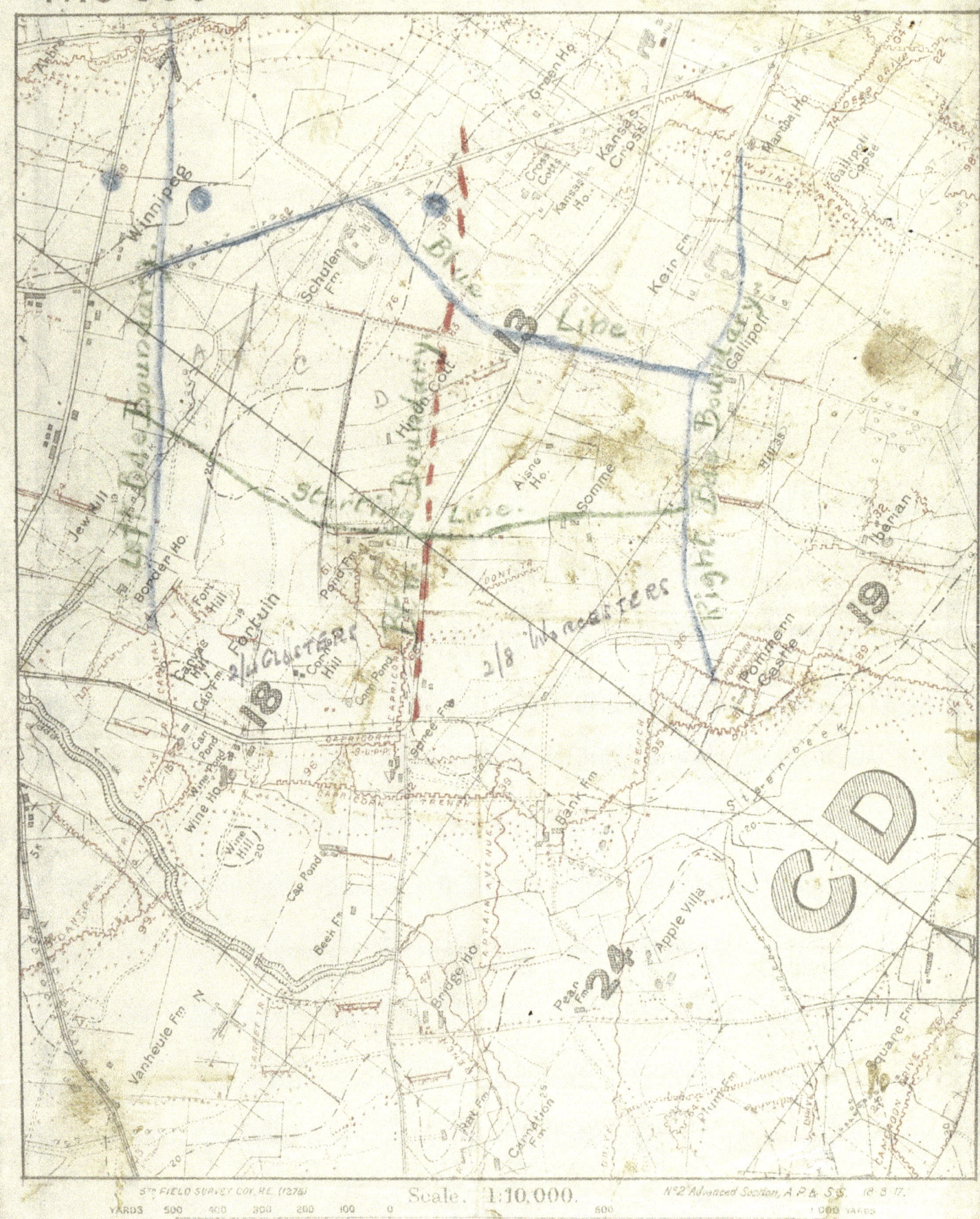

Message Form.

..........................Division.

Map reference or mark own position on Map at back.

I am at..

I am at..and am consolidating.

I am at..and have consolidated.

I need :—Ammunition.
        Bombs.
        Rifle Grenades.
        Water.
        Very lights.
        Stokes shells.

Enemy forming up for counter-attack at..

I am in touch with..................on Right / Left at..

I am not in touch on Right. / Left.

Am being shelled from..

I estimate my present strength at..................rifles.

Hostile { Battery / Machine Gun / Trench Mortar } active at....................

Time   a.m. (p.m.)   Name..................................

Date..................................   Platoon............Company............

Place..................................   Battalion..................................

APPENDIX to WAR DIARY.   AUGUST 1917.

2/4th Bn Gloucestershire Regiment.

	Offs.	O.R.		Offs.	O.R.
EFFECTIVE STRENGTH. August 1st	39	964.	August 31st.	34.	679.
RATION STRENGTH. "	30	894	"	22.	569.

EXPLANATION OF DIFFERENCE.

Reinforcements received.

	Offs.	O.R.
Joined	4	-
Rejoined	-	23.
TOTAL INCREASE	4	23.

Casualties.

	Offs.	O.R.
Evac.Sick.		61
Killed in Action	4	47
Wounded " "	5	152
Missing		33
Accid.Wounded		2
To.Base Depot		6
Transferred:-		
R.E.		3
61Div.H.Q.		1
183 L.T.M.B.		2
Base D.T.		1
	9	308.

	Offs.	O.R.
NET DECREASE.	5	285.

MAP SHOWING
: : BARRAGE LINES

Scale 1:10560

Secret No MS 91

E

2·20

·21
5·13
3 ·38
5·5

1·38
1·30
1·22
14

WAR DIARY

2/4th Battⁿ Gloucestershire Regᵗ

— Sept. 1917. — — Vol. 18. —

WAR DIARY
INTELLIGENCE SUMMARY.
(Erase heading not required.)

Army Form C. 2118.

Place	Date	Hour	Summary of Events and Information	Remarks and references to Appendices
BRANDHOEK	Sep. 1.		Resting and refitting	
	2.		do	
	3.		Coy. training	
	4.		do	
	5.		do	
	6.		do	
	7.		do	
	8.		Bn. moved to GOLDFISH CHATEAU Camp, arriving 7.30 p.m.	
	9.		Bn. relieved 2/6th Royal Warwicks in left Subsect. relief being complete by 7.45 p.m. The Sussannah Firing Line taken over by 153 & 154 Trench Bunker from 1/6 Lo Bucks 2/6 Dragoons, Rhine Farm (Boesw) and 3/4 Bhoova (Rifle Bgde Batty) taken over under orders from B.S.C. 15th by 1st Bde. Coming under orders of B.S.C. 15th by 1st Bde. Sussannah Heavy Artillery shelled.	
	10.	4 p.m.	Attack by 15th Bde on the Geneva on H/42 35, Zero being 4 p.m. The attack was successful prior to Heavy Hos.Line Heavy shelling put in on both sides Losses Artillery Formations by Reserve Bosches on RO.7/R.21/5. P.P.O. area. 100 Shells being used. Bn. relieved by 2 Coys 2/6 Bucks and 2 Coys 27 Dragoons.	

WAR DIARY
or
INTELLIGENCE SUMMARY.
(Erase heading not required.)

Army Form C. 2118.

Instructions regarding War Diaries and Intelligence Summaries are contained in F. S. Regs., Part II. and the Staff Manual respectively. Title pages will be prepared in manuscript.

Place	Date	Hour	Summary of Events and Information	Remarks and references to Appendices
	11.		Bn. moved to YPRES NORTH arriving 2am 12th inst.	
	12.		Bathing and resting	
	13.		Bn. moves to BRANDHOEK the 3 Coys. gone being employed by Corps.	
	14.		Bn. moved to WATOU to 2 areas, taking over camps at G.15a.0.1 (Ref Sheet 28) from 2nd South African Regimental Camp reached at 9.30am.	
	15.		Training.	
	16.		Brigade Athletic Sports. Divined.	
	17.		Bn. marched to NORTHHOUDT to 3 area. Camp between arial ZEVEKOTEN - WATOU - WINNEZEELE - OUDEZEELE - HARDIFORT. Billeting Parties sent on by 4.15 pm.	
	18.		Bn. marched to CASSEL Stn. and Entrained at 2.30pm for YPRES arriving 10.15pm. Marched to billets in SIMENCOURT arriving 2.15am. Route - Railway Crossing DAINVILLE - BERN AVILLE	
	19.		Resting	
	20.		Training	
	21.		Do	
	22.		Do	

WAR DIARY
or
INTELLIGENCE SUMMARY
(Erase heading not required.)

Army Form C. 2118.

Place	Date	Hour	Summary of Events and Information	Remarks and references to Appendices
	23.		Church Parade in the morning. Bn. marched to ST NICHOLAS CAMP at B.N.C. (Rd. Sheet 57b) leaving SIMENCOURT at 2.15 pm. Route: BERNEVILLE - DAINVILLE - Railway Group. DAINVILLE - FT AMIENS - Railway Group. ST NICHOLAS. Bn. arrived at 5.30 taking over Camp from 2/F Hanover.	
	24.		Bn. left for LEY DROUN T. GREENLAND HILL Slm. relieving 10th West Yorks 17th Division. R Coy - Blake. (HQ.O.O. Sheet 57b) Relieved front to civil avenue Relief completed 10.30 pm.	
	25.		Very quiet day. Line stores nearby trench mortar activity. Work on trenches. Roy. River.	
	26.		Trench mortar strong covered me to the 50 line	
	27.		Quiet day. Took R 10 of enemy LIEUT BIRD [...] enemy post and very heavily shelled, had returned to no mans land. Casualties - Pickett BIRD + 1 OR wounded.	
	28.		18th Division [...]	
	29.		Several trench mortar shots. Op lay by enemy. 3rd enemy [...] bombardment on my right Bn. by trench mortars + all calibres and artillery. Report engineer and St. Desk up, no enemy action known. Relieving Front Gradually extended [...] flank. Eventually Aying down Camp TROM, Gouv [...]	

Army Form C. 2118.

WAR DIARY
or
INTELLIGENCE SUMMARY.
(Erase heading not required.)

Place	Date	Hour	Summary of Events and Information	Remarks and references to Appendices
	30.		Heavy & close fire kept up thro' operation caused - 20% casualties - 10 ofrs & 150 of wounded. Text. Summ day. Bn relieved by 2/6 Gloster regn being completed by 10.35 p.m. Bn marched into billets at Reninghe.	
			Sd Stanbury Capt.	
			Commanding 2/4 Gloster	

APPENDIX B

Report on Operations Aug 27th 1917

The task of assembly for the above operations proved a difficult one owing to the very dark night and heavy rain which had made the going very bad.

On the way up to my battle head quarters - CAPRICORN KEEP - I learned that the left Coy had become split into two parts owing to heavy shelling and casualties on Number 6 Track. I saw the company commander at 6 Gloster H.Q. and he told me that he would have no difficulty in getting the rear half of the company into position and that the front half were already up in the line in their place. Soon after my arrival at CAPRICORN KEEP the company commander - Lieut HALL - reported with one of his platoon commanders 2/Lt HADLEY. I understood from what he said that he had found the rear half of his company and I sent him off at once to put them into position. From that time

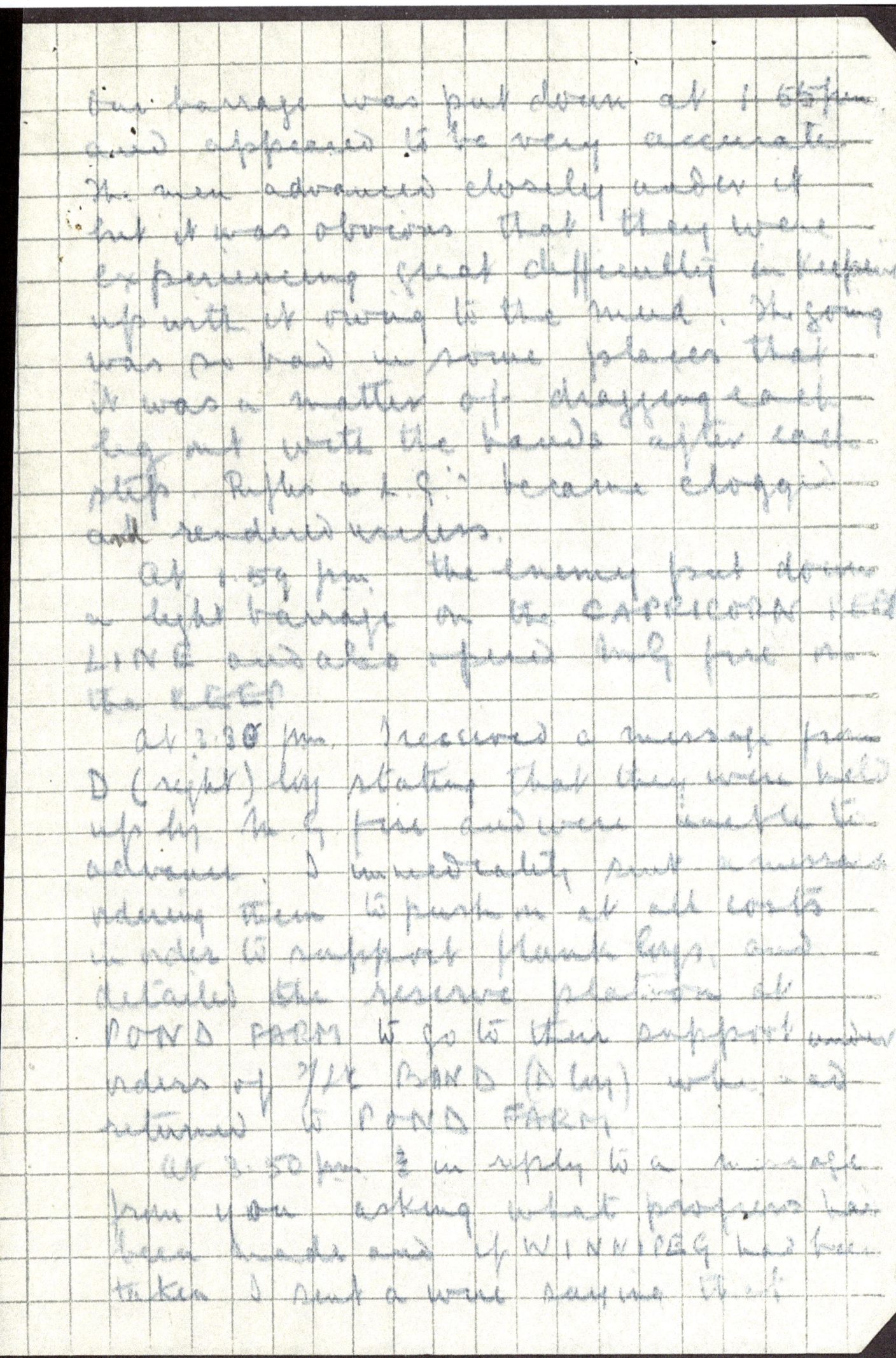

Our barrage was put down at 1.55 pm and appeared to be very accurate. The men advanced closely under it but it was obvious that they were experiencing great difficulty in keeping up with it owing to the mud. The going was so bad in some places that it was a matter of dragging each leg out with the hands after each step. Rifles + L.G.'s became clogged and rendered useless.

At 1.59 pm. the enemy put down a light barrage on the CAPRICORN RESERVE LINE and also opened MG fire on the KEEP.

At 2.30 pm. I received a message from D (right) Coy stating that they were held up by M.G. fire and were unable to advance. I immediately sent a runner ordering them to push on at all costs in order to support flank Coys and detailed the reserve platoon at POND FARM to go to their support under orders of 2/Lt BAND (A Coy) who had returned to POND FARM.

At 2.50 pm ? in reply to a message from you asking what progress had been made and if WINNIPEG had been taken I sent a wire saying that if

onwards I received no communication from the left Coy at all. This was due to the fact that a large swamp separated us and it was impossible to get runners through. It came to light afterwards the operation that the two platoons of this Coy referred to either went astray again or were never found by OC Coy, at any rate they did not take part in the action and appear to have been in the support line the whole time.

The other companies got into position well. One platoon of my reserve company was attached to the left Coy - A Coy - as I thought that their task would be the most difficult. Two platoons of the reserve company were at CAPRICORN KEEP and one at POND FARM SOMEWHERE

The state of the ground was very bad indeed and the men had to lie in shell holes up to their knees in water. I considered that the going would be so bad as to necessitate a slower rate of advance of the barrage but was informed that it could not be changed.

sent back to you shortly afterwards in accordance with instructions received.

By 5:30 pm about 12 wounded had arrived at the KEEP, heavily sniped at on the way. These were evacuated as soon as possible. Enemy artillery & m.g. fire was still heavy and there was a great deal of sniping.

At 6 pm the situation was unchanged and there was still no report from the left. By a message was received from you ordering reorganization and another attack, calling on the Support Battalion ~~to support~~ to take over the old line.

At 6.15 pm this message was cancelled and an order was received ordering me to dig in from where we were in touch with left Div to POND & QUARRIES.

At 6.20 pm OC centre Coy & Coy reports to me stating respective strengths were thus 12 O.R. and 30 O.R. respectively. At the same time BM 442 was received ordering me to establish myself in HINDU COT calling on me as two Coys of 6 platoons and working in conjunction with left Div to establish myself on the line WINNIPEG - HINDU

COTT. I therefore sent a message to B/Ktns asking for one company to reinforce the left Coy and 1 Coy to come to CAPRICORN KEEP as reserve. At the same time I ordered my 3 reserve platoons to reinforce my centre and right.

From 7.30 approx to 9 pm there was artillery barrage fire on both sides. At 10 pm an order was received that B/Ktns would take over command night 27/28. 4th platoons having established the line HINDU COTT to left Div. A post was established at HINDU COTT and orders to the above effect sent to left Coy by runners and patrols who however failed to find them owing to the swamps referred to above.

Centre & right Coys were relieved but two platoons of B Coy were unable to get out before dawn and are still at POND GALLERIES. No officers or men of the left company supporting platoon attached to have returned. This company as stated above never received its relief orders and must be still in the line.

no news had been received of left or centre company but that right Coy was held up by M.G. fire.

At 4 pm the centre company reported that they had failed to take their objectives owing to M.G. fire and the mud and had been forced to withdraw with heavy casualties. I therefore ordered the supporting platoon at POND FARM (which was about to move forward) to stand by and I sent a message stating that centre & right were now forced to withdraw and had suffered heavy casualties — asking for instructions.

At 4.30 pm a message was received from Bde Signal Officer asking for situation report and instructing me to man new line and old line. A reply was sent as that right + centre were held up.

At 5 pm a message was received by runner timed 4.5pm stating that artillery was being turned on again and ordering the line to be established firmly in north of SCHULER GALLERIES. As this was my last message I direw myporn to consolidate on present ground.

At 5.15 pm 2 R.E. parties reported to take tasks forward. These were

exclusive of left Coy which it is
known lost. 2 officers wounded.
Approximate casualties are:—
  3 officers
  180 O.R.

I consider that the failure to take
the objectives was chiefly due to
the mud and to the men having
to lie in water for 2 hours prior
to the attack. I feel confident that
only for this the objectives would
have been taken & held in spite
of M.G. fire.

The men are very much exhausted
and in need of a hot meal and
dry clothes especially socks.

28/8/17   R.E. Poulton Lieut Col
            Comdg Y & L / Yorkers

2/4th Bn Gloucestershire Regiment.

APPENDIX "A" TO WAR DIARY.   SEPTEMBER 1917.

	Offs.	O.R.		Offs.	O.R.
EFFECTIVE STRENGTH Septem.1st.	34	679	September 30th	31.	644.
RATION STRENGTH " "	22.	569	" "	24.	612.

EXPLANATION OF DIFFERENCE.

	Offs.	O.R.	
Reinforcements received.	-	40.	Rejoined.

Casualties.

	Offs.	O.R.
Evac.Sick.	1	46
Evac.Wounded.	1	25
Tfd.T.M.B.		2
To.I.B.D. Unfit.		1
Tfd.2ndS.M.F.Co.R.E.		1
Seconded.	1	-
	3.	75.

	Offs.	O.R.
NET DECREASE.	3	35.

CONFIDENTIAL

Vol 18

2/4th BATT. THE GLOUCESTERSHIRE REGIMENT

G.A

WAR DIARY

OCTOBER 1917.

VOL. 18.

WAR DIARY
INTELLIGENCE SUMMARY.
(Erase heading not required.)

Army Form C. 2118.

Place	Date	Hour	Summary of Events and Information	Remarks and references to Appendices
	1		Left support left section. GREENLANDS HILL section; working parties	
	2			
	3			
	4		Relieved by 2/4 R. BERKS. Relief complete 11:50 p.m. 80 marches to LANCASTER CAMP AREAS	
	5		Resting; cleaning up; baths	
	6		Training; range	
	7		" " — very wet	
	8		" "	
	9		" "	
	10		— Lt. Col. R.E. BOULTON left for England for six months. Transfer; Major	
			D.G. GUERNSEY assumed command	
	11		Working parties; training	
	12		" "	
	13		Training	
	14		Church Parade	
	15		Training; baths	
	16		Relieved 2/7 R. Warwicks in left sub-section. Right parties. Relief complete 11:20 p.m.	
	17		Very Quiet	
	18		" "	

WAR DIARY
or
INTELLIGENCE SUMMARY.

Army Form C. 2118.

Place	Date	Hour	Summary of Events and Information	Remarks and references to Appendices
	19		Quiet day.	
	20		Artillery more active	
	21		Quiet day.	
	22		Quiet day: relieved by 2/6 Glosters: relief complete 9.20 p.m. A Coy moved into left support; B + D Coys in HERTH TRENCH, A + C in COLTICARZ.	
	23		Wet day: working parties: heavy artillery fire at 11 p.m. during raid by 184 Bde.	
	24		Raid by Bty. (2 officers + 50 OR) in conjunction with 2/7 Warw. astride the Railway cutting. Attack was launched at 3.50 p.m. after a Division barrage of 20 minutes duration. The raiders were held up by insufficient gaps in the wire and dry rifle fire. Many casualties were inflicted on the enemy. Hostile artillery fire was very heavy and the trenches were badly damaged. Our casualties were 2 killed + 24 wounded. Bombardment of enemy lines at 11 p.m. during raid by 184 Bde.	Operation Orders and report attached
	25		Wet day: working parties	
	26			
	28		Relieved 2/6 Glosters in left front line: relief complete 7.30 p.m.	
	29		Quiet day; raid by party of 2/6 Glosters 2 officers + 53 OR. from our left front	
	30		trench. Mortar and artillery activity	
	31			

D.J. Barnsley
Captain 2/7th Bn. Gloucester Regt.

2/4th Bn Gloucestershire Regiment.

APPENDIX TO WAR DIARY.   OCTOBER 1917.

	Offs.	O.R.		Offs.	O.R.
EFFECTIVE STRENGTH October 1st	31.	644	OCTOBER 31st	34	860
RATION STRENGTH " "	24.	612.	" "	24	701.

EXPLANATION OF DIFFERENCE.

	Offs.	O.R.		Offs.	O.R.
REINFORCEMENTS RECEIVED	5	278		5	278.

CASUALTIES.

	Offs.	O.R.
Killed in Action		5
Died of Wounds		2
Missing		1
Wounded in Action	1.	14
Evac. Sick.		35
Accid. Injured		1
To England	1	-
" " (Commission)		3
To I.B.D. Unfit		1
	2	62

			Offs.	O.R.
			2	62
NET INCREASE			3	216

I am entirely satisfied with the way in which the men went over. They were in good heart and were well led by their section leaders, 2/Lieut. R.J.C. NURSE, Sgt. FLEMING, and Sgt. SALMON.

L/Cpl. Gough showed good initiative and leadership in directing the discharge of P Bombs during the withdrawal.

The Raid took place at an earlier date than had been expected and apart from an examination of a hasty made model, there was no time for any special training, but in spite of this, Lieut. W.G. SHIPWAY was able to organise and instruct his party and it is entirely due to his good leadership and example that the men went forward as they did, and were successfully withdrawn. I am confident that, had the wire not been so formidable, they would have successfully carried out the whole programme.

I should like to put on record my thanks to the Officer Commanding, 3/6th Glosters, for so readily affording every facility and much useful co-operation in the preliminaries and carrying out of the Raid.

                                    (Signed) D.G. BARNSLEY.
                                              Lieut. Colonel,
24.10.17.   Commanding 2/4th Battn. Gloucestershire Regt.

N.C.O's names and numbers.

301647 Sergt. FLEMING W.
302784 Sergt. SALMON W.
302872 L/Sgt. GOUGH C.

2/4th Battalion Gloucestershire Regiment.

R E P O R T   O N   R A I D   24.10.17.

183rd Inf. Bde.

Herewith my Report on Raid carried out by "B" Company, 2/4th Glosters on afternoon 24.10.17. Copy of Operation Orders has already been forwarded.

The Raiding Party consisting of 2 Officers and 51 other ranks assembled at hour ordered and were accomodated in dug-outs in CINEMA and COLD ALLEY.

At 3.30 p.m. they left assembly place and moved down to jumping off place (head of T Sap, I.14.a.6.7) which was reached without casualty at 3.40 p.m. F.L. trenches were found to be damaged and shelling was fairly heavy.

Scaling ladders had been prepared and 3 gaps cut in our wire at head of T Sap on night 23rd/24th.

Our shrapnel barrage came down at Zero plus 1.30 and 30 secs. after O.C.Raid ordered party over the parapet. The men doubled in 2 waves as follows:-

    Z Party   Y Party   X Party   1st Wave.
        Parapet Party   2nd Wave.

I regret to report that 3 casualties were sustained from our barrage, which according to statement by the officers of the party, appeared to be down on lines marked black on attached map. It will be noticed from this that part of the Hun front line had escaped our barrage and on advancing across NO MANS LAND the Raiding party came under rifle fire from this point and also under M.G.fire from their left front. Enemy could be seen manning their parapet and at least 8 were counted near junction of WURZEL and front line. Under cover of rifle and L.G.fire the party continued to advance and got to about 15x from the enemy wire. This was found to be from 10x to 15x thick and with the exception of what appeared to be a narrow zig-zag path about a yard wide, opposite WURZEL, there was no opening for the raiders to get through. O.C.Raid therefore disposed his party in shell holes and continued engaging the enemy with a brisk rifle and L.G.fire. The enemy appeared daring and did not hesitate to show themsleves - one man in particular being noticed kneeling on the parapet. Their shooting was not good and our party scored several hits. The Lewis Gunners claimed to have knocked out a light M.G. or automatic rifle which opened fire about I.14.a.95.95. Bombs were also thrown by both sides, several being seen to burst in the enemy's F.L. Lieut. Shipway then noticed that Raiding Party on his right (S. of cutting) was retiring and he fired recall signal (Red Very Light) This was at 4.5 pm. Under cover of P Bombs and rifle fire the party fell back, by sections to T Sap. The "All in" signal was sent up at 4.11 pm., Lt. Shipway and Sergt. Salmon being the last to return.

CASUALTIES.   Killed .. 2 o/ranks.
                Wounded ... 4 "   )all brought in.

AEROPLANE.   An enemy plane flew low over our line from 4.15 pm. to 4.50 pm. dropping white Very Lights alternately N & S of the cutting.

COLOURED LIGHTS   Double Reds were sent up by enemy as the party assaulted and double greens on withdrawal.

The Relay system of Stretcher Bearers worked well, though fortunately their services were not extensively required.

All signal communication by wire, between my position, Rgt. H.Q.@INEMA) and assembly and checking station (Centre Coy Coy. H.Q. (CUPID SUPPORT) was cut early on during the enemy's retaliation to our bombardment from Zero to Zero plus 20. Communication by runners was difficult as CUPID, COLD ALLEY and CINEMA all received much attention.

2/4th Battalion Gloucestershire Regiment.

SECRET.   OPERATION ORDERS No. 91.   Copy No. 1

By Lieut. Colonel D.G. BARNSLEY, Comdg.   IN The Field, 23.10.17.

Ref. FAMPOUX Trench sheet and Air Photo Map.13.L.A. 2448.

1. On the 24th inst. two parties of about 2 Officers and 50 men each will raid the enemy's Front Line and Support Trenches, North and South of the Railway Cutting.
   1st Party- 4th Glosters will raid North of the Railway Cutting.
   2nd Party- 7th Worcesters will raid South of the Railway Cutting.
   with the object of:-
   (a) Destroying dug-outs.
   (b) Inflicting casualties on the enemy.

2. Point of entry for 4th Glosters will be at I.14.b.10.80., the junction of WURZEL C.T. with Front Line.
   Point of entry for 7th Worcesters will be at I.14.a.95.50., and I.14.a.90.00.

3. There will be a previous intense bombardment by the Corps Heavy Artillery, 61st Artillery and 15th Div. Artillery, from Zero to Zero plus 30.
   During this period the Front Line and Saps opposite the trenches to be raided will be cleared of all troops.
   There will be a pause of 30 minutes during which the assaulting troops will move into their jumping off positions.
   At Zero plus 40 the Divisional Artilleries, Medium Trench Mortars, and Light Trench Mortars will form a box barrage round the area to be raided and the infantry will assault.

4. The Dividing Line between Battalions will be the RAILWAY CUTTING inclusive to the 4th Glosters.
   The 4th Glosters will not go further North up the enemy's trenches than 80^x beyond the junction of C.T. and Firing Line at I.8.d.05.35.

5. Smoke will be put out on both flanks of the assault if the wind is favourable.

6. **METHOD OF ATTACK.**
   The attacking party will consist of three Storm parties and one parapet party. These will be composed as follows:-
   X.(Right Party).   1 N.C.O.
                      2 Lewis Gunners with Gun.
                      8 Bayonet men.
   Y.(Centre Party). 1 Officer.
                      14 Bayonet men.
   Z.(Left Party).   1 N.C.O.
                      12 Bayonet men.
   Parapet Party.
                      O.C. Raid.
                      1 Runner.
                      6 Bayonet Men.
                      4 Stretcher Bearers with two stretchers.
                      2 Wire cutters.
   The raiding party will move down via CAMEL AV. - CROOK ALLEY - CINEMA ER. - COLD ALLEY - CRANK ALLEY to Front Line.
   They will report at Advanced B.H.Q. (at present Centre Coy.H.Q.) at Zero minus 15.
   At Zero plus 30, O.C.Raid will move his party down Front Line and will occupy Head of T.SAP which will form the jumping off place.
   The assault will be launched from here at Zero plus 40.
   X Party will turn right at point of entry and will deal with dug-out A and any further dug-outs or saps in Trench, leading South to RAILWAY CUTTING and along RAILWAY CUTTING.
   Y Party will proceed straight up WURZEL C.T. and after detaching two men each to form stops at places marked on map (attached), will turn left and deal with all dug-outs in trench leading to Area H and in area H itself.

6. Cont'd.
Z.Party will turn Left at Point of Entry, and will work North along German Front Line, dealing with dug-outs,"B","C""D" & "E".

The parapet Party will remain near Point of Entry, under immediate Command of O.C.Raid, and will send back any prisoners. They will also see that the enemy does not come over the open, and will shovel earth and push sandbags into the trench to facilitate exit.

7. WITHDRAWAL.
The raiding party will remain in the enemy trenches not longer than 20 minutes. The signal for withdrawal will be a succession of Red Very Lights fired from British Front Line, near end of T.Sap. This will be taken up by the O.C.Raid and section leaders by a succession of short whistle blasts. All parties will at once make their way back to our own lines. The men with wire cutters will improve gaps in enemy's wire to facilitate withdrawal. The party will re-assemble at the original assembly place (Adv.Battn.H.Q. in CINEMA TR.) where leaders will check and report to 2/Lieut. Harrison.

O.C.Raid will report "All in" at Adv. Report Centre.

8. Artillery will continue to fire on all T.M.E. and M.G.E. for ten minutes after raiders have been reported "All in".

9. No documents, letters, papers, orders or any article by which the enemy might get an identification, will be carried by any of the raiders.

10. DRESS & EQUIPMENT.
Equipment will not be worn.
Each bayonet man will carry:- (a) 30 rounds S.A.A. in the right jacket pocket, (b) one Mills Bomb in each breast pocket, (c) one P.Bomb in left jacket pocket.

All leaders will carry whistles and watches.

Wire cutting party will carry wire cutter, rifle and bayonet, and 30 rounds S.A.A.

Three bayonet men of parapet party will carry one shovel each.

11. COMMUNICATION.
Battn. Signal Officer will arrange for an Advanced Report Centre to be opened at present Right Coy.H.Q.(CUPID SUPPORT) and will lay a direct wire from there to Adv. Battn.H.Q. in CINEMA TR.

Telephones will be installed at Stations forward of BattnH.Q at Zero.

12. Battn.Signal Officer will be responsible that all watches are synchronized at 9.15 am. and 12.15 p.m.

13. The 6th Glosters will arrange to marshall and escort all prisoners to Bde.H.Q.

14. Every effort will be made to bring back wounded but no one except stretcher bearers will bring casualties in until after the withdrawal signal.

Evacuation of wounded will be made through Left.Battn.R.A.P. 4th Glosters and 6th Glosters will each provide a party of 12 Stretcher bearers to report to Quarry A.D.S. one hour before Zero. M.O. 4th Glosters will assist at this A.D.S. and will arrange for a bearer relay post to be established in South End of CALICO TR. and an advanced post near T.Sap.

15. Programmes of artillery, Trench Mortars and M.G's will be issued later.

16. Zero Hour will be notified later to all concerned by code set out in Div. Circular G.C.9/2 dated 10.10.17.

P.T.O.

17.   Until Zero no mention of this operation will take place on the wire.

18.   ACKNOWLEDGE.

                        (Signed) H.D.CUMMING.
                            Lieut. & A/Adjutant.
                    2/4th Battalion Gloucestershire Regiment.

Issued at ....

        Copies to: No. 1   War Diary.
                           2   File.
                           3   C.O.
                           4   Adjutant.
                           5   O.C."B"Coy.
                           6   183rd Inf. Bde.
                           7   O.C.2/6th Glosters.
                           8   O.C.2/7th Worcesters.

1st Bn Gloucestershire Regiment.

95/19

WAR DIARY.

Volume 19.

November 1917

Army Form C. 2118.

WAR DIARY
or
INTELLIGENCE SUMMARY.
(Erase heading not required.)

Instructions regarding War Diaries and Intelligence Summaries are contained in F.S. Regs., Part II. and the Staff Manual respectively. Title pages will be prepared in manuscript.

Place	Date	Hour	Summary of Events and Information	Remarks and references to Appendices
	Nov. 1		Quiet morning. Heavy Artillery fire on Left Coy 4 – 4.30 p.m. Quiet night.	
	2		Intermittent Artillery and T.M. fire on both sides.	
	3		Quiet morning. Practice Barrage by Artillery on Left and Centre Coy 4 p.m. – 4.8 p.m. Relieved by 2/6th Glos. relief complete 7.45 p.m. Battn moved into Left Support. A.Coy CADIZ – C.Coy COLT, B–D Coy LEMON. Working Parties.	
	4		" A Coy took over D post from 2/6 Glos.	
	5		"	
	6		Working Parties.	
	7		"	
	8		" C. Coy took over C. Strong Point from 2/6 Glos.	
	9		Brigade went into Reserve at ARRAS. Battn. relief complete 7.45 p.m. Battn went into billets at LEVIS BARRACKS.	
	10		Fatigues & working parties.	
	11		Church Parade – Baths.	
	12		Cleaning up & refitting.	
	13		Working Parties & training.	

WAR DIARY or **INTELLIGENCE SUMMARY.**

(Erase heading not required.)

Army Form C. 2118.

Place	Date	Hour	Summary of Events and Information	Remarks and references to Appendices
	14		Guards, Fatigues & Working Parties.	
	15		Training & Working Parties.	
	16		Brigade musketry meeting.	
	17		"	
	18		Guards, Fatigues & Working Parties.	
	19		Brigade Boxing Competitions	
	20		Training & Working Parties.	
	21		Bn. relieved 2/5 R Warwicks in Left Front Line GREENLAND HILL Sector. D. Coy LEFT. A. Coy. CENTRE - B. Coy. RIGHT - C. Coy. SUPPORT. Relief completed at 8.40 pm without incident. Quiet night.	
	22		Fine Day. Artillery & T.M's active on both sides. Support lines & C.T's Shelled intermittently. 1 O.R. wounded.	
	23		"	
	24		Fine day, quiet. Considerable hostile artillery fire.	
	25		Fine day, quiet. 1 O.R. killed.	
	26		" Artillery & T.M's active. 3 O.R. wd.	
	27		Heavy shelling of CORK SUPPORT & C.T's. Relief by 1/6 Glos when in progress was cancelled as orders had been received of a Divisional Relief	

WAR DIARY
or
INTELLIGENCE SUMMARY.
(Erase heading not required.)

Army Form C. 2118.

Place	Date	Hour	Summary of Events and Information	Remarks and references to Appendices
	Nov. 28		Batn relieved by 6 CAMERONS (15 Bde) Relief completed 2 p.m. Bn marched to ARRAS. Orders received for move to BAPAUME area.	
	29		Baths. Preparations for move.	
	30		Marched to DAINVILLE, leaving ARRAS 6.50 a.m. Entrained to BAPAUME. Original intention being to march from there to BAPAUME. Bapaume the orders were changed and the Division transferred to 2nd Corps as enemy had broken through near GOUZEAUCOURT. Division was bussed up the line immediately in order to RUYAULCOURT. From there Bn marched to TRESCAULT and encamped on the S.E. corner of HAVRINCOURT WOOD about Q. 15. a. 7. 5. arriving 6.0 p.m. GUARDS counter-attacked during evening and at night and regained part of lost ground.	

W T N---- A. Captain
for O.C. 2/5 Bn Gloucester Regt

CONFIDENTIAL

Vol 20
183/61

2/4th BATTN THE GLOUCESTERSHIRE REGIMENT.

WAR DIARY.

G.20
DECEMBER, 1917.

VOL. 20.

Army Form C. 2118.

WAR DIARY
or
INTELLIGENCE SUMMARY.
(Erase heading not required.)

Place	Date	Hour	Summary of Events and Information	Remarks and references to Appendices
HAVRINCOURT WOOD	December 1		B's reconcentrated in Huts. Brigade under orders of G.O.C. 20th Div. Officers reconnoitred forward area in the morning. Orders received at 3 pm for B's to move off at 4.30 pm into the line. Relieved details of 9th Surreys and 11th K.R.R. in front line, 16 d. and 22 a. (reference GONNELIEU map) (Centre on left, Wrexden on right. Guards Division on right of 7th Brigade.) Bn HR. established in LA VACQUERIE. The relief was successfully accomplished under great difficulties as the line was held by remains of eight companies and had only been retaken in the previous day. Heavy shelling during up rounds and relief. The M.O. (Capt. ROBSON) was killed and the R.S.M. and 8 O.R. wounded (all Bn. HQ personnel). There was no wire in front of the line taken over & there was a shortage of bombs and 2 C.T's led from the German line into our LA VACQUERIE was heavily shelled during the night.	
	2		Heavy and continuous shelling of LA VACQUERIE. Bombing fights took place intermittently at junction of C.T's joining our front line with the enemy (HINDENBURG) line. 2 prisoners were taken by right Coy (Bdy) in the Sunken road in 21 d. At 2.30 pm enemy put down a heavy barrage and attacked 6 Platoon on our left causing withdrawal of part of their line and leaving a gap of about 30" with the enemy in the same trench. An over-line S.Waterloo came up and attacked this part at night but failed owing to their being shot where trench was met...	

Army Form C. 2118.

WAR DIARY
or
INTELLIGENCE SUMMARY.
(Erase heading not required.)

Instructions regarding War Diaries and Intelligence Summaries are contained in F. S. Regs., Part II. and the Staff Manual respectively. Title pages will be prepared in manuscript.

Place	Date	Hour	Summary of Events and Information	Remarks and references to Appendices
	Dec 3		4/c day spent in the front line and in C.T.'s joining enemy front line with own. There was heavy shelling of back area during the night	are appended
	-4		Enemy attack on LA VACQUERIE – his fourth attempt Heavy shelling – no enemy attack in Brigade front. Firm fairly day	
	-5		Heavy shelling of front line, posts and C.T.'s and back areas. Our artillery replies effectively, a large number of guns have been brought up. Relieved by 4 R Berks at 7.30 p.m. Bn withdrawn to Bde MR in VILLERS PLOUICH and became reserve Bn.	
	-6	4.30 am	Relieved at 4.30 am by 2/5 Gloster's withdrew to camp in HAVRINCOURT WOOD. Great casualties for period	
			Officers killed Capt W.G HUTCHINGS Lt. K J.G. BRADFORD Capt ROBSON BAME Lt W.G SHIPWAY 2/Lt G.E. BAND 2/Lt F.R RAWLINGS	
			O.R. Killed Missing Wounded 20 121 88	
	-7		Working party of 10 O.R. on new reserve line	
	-8			
	-9		Inspection and address by Major G. O.C Division, who congratulated the Bn. on the fine work performed in recent battle. Heavy shelling of camp in the morning, and again at night.	

WAR DIARY
or
INTELLIGENCE SUMMARY.
(Erase heading not required.)

Army Form C. 2118.

Instructions regarding War Diaries and Intelligence Summaries are contained in F. S. Regs., Part II. and the Staff Manual respectively. Title pages will be prepared in manuscript.

Place	Date	Hour	Summary of Events and Information	Remarks and references to Appendices
	10th		Battn. in the afternoon. Battalion reorganised into 2 Companies — Total 15 platoons. Brigade relief; Bn took over Reserve line from 7/Wilts; Bn. HQ in LINCOLN AVENUE Q. 12.c.6.6.	See Appendix 2
	11th		Quiet day - work on trenches very wet.	
	12th		Intermittent shelling of Reserve line	
	13th		ditto	
	14th		Relieved 6 platoons in left front line, Bn. HQ in FREM RAVINE. Relief complete 6.30 pm.	
	15th		Our artillery barrage between 6.30 & 7.30 am; known retaliation in support line and VILLAGE ROAD. Quiet morning. Desultory shelling in afternoon. Our artillery barrage again at 4.30.	
	16th		Artillery barrage between 6am and 7am. Quiet day; relieved by 1/5 platoons 1c 1/5 a shot complete 9.15 pm. Bn. moved back to HAVRINCOURT WOOD.	
	17th		Cleaning up - bath.	
	18th		Working parties	
	19th		training	

WAR DIARY
or
INTELLIGENCE SUMMARY.

(Erase heading not required.)

Army Form C. 2118.

Place	Date	Hour	Summary of Events and Information	Remarks and references to Appendices
	20th		Brigade relief. M̄s relieved 7/5 Yorks in front line; left instruction M̄s H.Q. in FARM RAVINE. Relief complete 15:30 p.m.	See Appendix 4
	21st		Quiet day. Very cold and heavy frost	
	22nd		Front and support line still in running. Relieved by ANSON M̄s and 2 — R.M.L.I. — relief complete 6:30 p.m. M̄s moved to HAVRINCOURT WOOD	See Appendix 5.
	23rd		Moved to MANANCOURT. — arrived 11:10 p.m.	See Appendix 6+7
	24th		Moved to BRAY-SUR-SOMME. M̄s less transport and 1 off and 100 ōr entrained at ETRICOURT at 2.15 p.m. — arrived PLATEAU S.G. 3:45 p.m. Marched to BRAY arriving 8:45 p.m. Lorries travelled by road empty owing to slippery state of road surface; started from arrival 6 p.m. Remainder of transport plus 1 officer and 100 ōr entrained 8 p.m.; arrived 2:30 a.m. Very wet day. Slippery state of roads caused by snow that made the move a very difficult one	See Appendix 8
	25th		Resting; cleaning up and refitting; talks	
	26th			
	27th		training	

Army Form C. 2118.

WAR DIARY
or
INTELLIGENCE SUMMARY.
(Erase heading not required.)

Instructions regarding War Diaries and Intelligence Summaries are contained in F.S. Regs., Part II. and the Staff Manual respectively. Title pages will be prepared in manuscript.

Place	Date	Hour	Summary of Events and Information	Remarks and references to Appendices
	28th		Training: Christmas celebrations. Fine frosty day.	
	29th		Training. Very cold.	
	30th		Church Parade :-	
	31st		Bn. moved by road to GUILLAUCOURT — started 8.25 a.m. arrived 1 p.m. next PLOY ART — MARGRONNIERES. Fine in am & early forenoon track wet at 7.30 p.m. Snow.	See appendix 9.

J.G. Ramsey
Lieut Col
Comndg 1/4th Bn Yorks Regt.

2/4th Battalion Gloucestershire Regt
OPERATION ORDERS No 100 Copy No 7
By Lieut Colonel D.G. BARNSLEY, Comdg.   2   9.12.17

SECRET

1. 2/4th Glosters will relieve 2/7th Worcesters tomorrow 10th December in the reserve line.

2. No 1 Coy. will relieve 'A' & 'B' Coys 2/7th Worcesters (Left) No 2 Coy. will relieve 'C' & 'D' Coys. 2/7th Worcesters (right).
Bn. H.Q. will move to Q.23.b.1.3.

3. One officer per Coy., one N.C.O. per platoon and one runner per Coy. will proceed to the reserve line tomorrow morning to take over. Runners will be sent back to guide relieving Coys.

4. The Bn. will march off from present camp as under:-
   No 1 Coy.   3.30 pm.
   No 2 "   3.35 pm.
   Bn H.Q.   3.40 pm.
An interval of 100x will be maintained between platoons.

5. Officers kits and mens blankets will be dumped in present camp under

Coy. arrangements. Transport Officer will arrange to collect as soon as possible.

6. Rations and water for consumption 11th and 12th inst will be sent tomorrow night to new Bn HQ. Coys. will be notified at what time to send rations parties.

7. Packs will be taken to the reserve line.

8. O.C. Rear party will be responsible for cleaning up camp.

9. ACKNOWLEDGE.

Issued at 8.45 p.m.

(Signed) S. J. STOTESBURY
Captain & Adjutant
2/4th Glosters.

Copy N° 1 War Diary
      2   C.O.
    3-4   O.C. Coys.
      5   Q.M. & T.O
      6   R.S.M.
      7   File
      8   183 Bde.

2/4th Battalion Gloucestershire Regt.

SECRET   OPERATION ORDERS No. 101   3

By Lieut. Colonel G.D. BARNSLEY, Comdg.   15.12.17

Reference 51c S.E.
           GONNELIEU Trench Map.

1. The 2/4th Glosters will be relieved by 2/5th Glosters on 16th inst; and night 16/17th inst.

2. After relief the 2/4th Glosters will move to HAVRINCOURT WOOD — route FIFTEEN RAVINE — direct.

3.   No. 1 Coy. 2/4th Glosters (Front Line) will be relieved by 'B' & 'D' Coys 2/5th Glosters; 'B' Coy taking over on the right and 'D' Coy on the Left.
       No. 2 Coy. 2/4th Glosters (Support Line) will be relieved by 'A' Coy. 2/5th Glosters.

4. Guides 1 per incoming platoon and 1 for each Coy. H.Q. will report at Bn. H.Q. at 3 pm.
    Total number of guides to be sent is as follows:—
      No 1 Coy ... 8 (6 platoons & 2 Coy. H.Q.)
      No 2 Coy ... 4 (3 "   1 ")
    Guides will proceed from Bn. H.Q. to

the Reserve Line where they will meet the incoming unit.

5. The following personnel of relieving Battn. will come into the line tomorrow morning.
    - 1 Officer per Coy.
    - 1 Signaller & 1 runner per Coy.
    - 4 Battalion runners.
    - 2 Observers.

6. Trench Stores will be carefully handed over and receipts (together with receipts for documents) sent to present Bn. H.Q. by 5 p.m. tomorrow.

7. R.S.M. will hand over 54 petrol tins at Bn. H.Q. Remainder of petrol tins will be carried out by Companies and dumped at Bn. H.Q. together with Lewis Guns, Lewis gun equipment and Company stores. These will be left in charge of the Provost Sergeant at Bn H.Q. and Transport Officer will send 2 Limbers to Bn H.Q. at 9 p.m. to collect same.

8. Details of new area will be arranged by Major Wyatt who will provide guides at the edge of the wood in Q.16.d.

9. Completion of relief will be wired to Bn HQ — Code word :- "JANE"

10. ACKNOWLEDGE.

(Signed) S.J. STOTESBURY
Captain & Adjutant
2/4th Bn Gloster Regt.

Issued at 7 pm.

Copies to :-

No 1	C.O.
2 & 3	O.C. Coys.
4	183 Bde
5	Rear H.Q.
6	QM. & T.O.
7	R.S.M.
8	File
9	War Diary

SECRET.

2/4th Battalion Gloucestershire Regiment.

OPERATION ORDERS NO. 102.

Copy No. 4

By Lt. Col. D.G. BARNSLEY, Comdg.   In the Field.   19.12.17.

1. The 2/4 Glosters will relieve 2/5 Glosters in LEFT SUBSECTION on December 20th.

2. Dispositions will be as sketch map attached.

3. No guides will be provided by 2/5 Glosters.

4. The Battalion will march off in the following order: No 1 Coy, No 2 Coy, Bn. H.Q.
   No. 1 Coy. will march off at 2.30pm.
   Route: FIFTEEN RAVINE. Intervals of 300 yards will be maintained between platoons.

5. The following will proceed to the line tomorrow-morning to take over:-
   1 Officer per Coy.   1 N.C.O. per platoon.
   1 N.C.O. from Bn.H.Q.   2 runners per Coy.
   2 runners from Bn.H.Q.   Nos. 1 of L.G. Teams.
   1 N.C.O. & 3 signallers per Coy.
   1 N.C.O. & 7 signallers from Bn H.Q.
   Personnel will parade at Bn. H.Q. under senior officer at 10am.
   N.C.Os. and runners will meet their companies at FARM RAVINE at 5.0pm.

6. One limber will be at Bn. H.Q. at 1.30pm. Lewis Guns and Lewis Gun equipment will be loaded by 2.0pm and the limber will proceed to the ration dump at FARM RAVINE where Coys. will draw their Lewis Guns on arrival.

7. Blankets and officers' valises will be dumped at Bn. H.Q. by 12 noon. Officers' mess baskets will be dumped at Bn. H.Q. by 2.0pm.

8. Two days rations and water will be taken up to Bn. H.Q. tomorrow night.

9. Taking over certificates will be forwarded to Bn. H.Q. by 12 noon 21st inst.

10. Relief complete will be sent to Bn. H.Q. by wire. Code word: MINCE PIES.

11. ACKNOWLEDGE.

                                (Signed) S.J. STOKESBURY.
                                         Captain and Adjutant.
                                         2/4th Gloucestershires.

Issued at 9.15pm.

          Copy No. 1   War Diary.
                   2   C.O.
                   3 - 4 OC Coys.
                   5   Q.M.
                   6   T.O.
                   7   R.S.M.
                   8   183 Inf. Bde.
                   9   2/5 Glosters.
                  10   File.

SECRET

2/4th Battalion Gloucestershire Regt.
OPERATION ORDERS No 103   5.
By Lieut Colonel D.G. BARNSLEY, Comdg.   22/12/17.

1. 2/4th Glosters will be relieved as under on the 22nd inst and night of 22/23rd.
   (a) One platoon of 'C' Coy. 2nd R.M. Bn. will take over from No 5 and No 6 platoons, No 2 Coy. 2/4th Glosters also Coy. H.Q.
   (NOTE:- Support Platoon No. 2 Coy 2/4th Glosters will not be relieved and may move out when front line relief is complete.)
   (b) Four platoons of 'A' Compy. ANSON Bn. will take over from four platoons of No 1 Coy. 2/4th Glosters also Coy. H.Q.
   (NOTE:- Boundary between ANSON & R.M. Bn will be RILEY AVENUE.)
   (c) Battalion H.Q. ANSON BATTN. will take over Battn H.Q. 2/4th Glosters.

2. After relief 2/4 Glosters will move to exactly the same camp as was vacated on 20th inst in HAVRINCOURT WOOD. - route:- FIFTEEN RAVINE and thence cross-country.

3. Guides.   From   For
   1 Platoon Guide } No 2 Coy.   'C' Coy 2nd R.M.Bn
   1 Coy. H.Q. —"— }

3. Cont. Guides

                                                From   For

    4 Platoon Guides   No 1 Coy.   A Coy ANSON
    1 Coy. H.Q. Guide

    1 Bn. H.Q. Guide   B.H.Q.   BHQ   ANSON

    4 Platoon Guides   Bn. H.Q.   D. Coy ANSON

4. All above guides will be provided with chits and will report to Lieut. Benton at Bn. H.Q. at 12.30 pm tomorrow 22nd inst.

5. Four limbers will be at ration dump at FARM RAVINE at 6 pm. for conveyance of Lewis Guns, Petrol Tins, and Company and H.Q. Stores.

6. Petrol tins and Company Stores are to be sent down to the ration dump by 2 pm.

7. Lewis Guns, Ammunition and equipment will be dumped at the ration dump, under charge of Sergt. Stevens, by outgoing platoons after being relieved.

8. Receipts for trench stores and

certificates to the effect that trenches were handed over in a clean and sanitary condition will be forwarded to Battn HQ by 12 noon.

9. Usual taking over parties will be coming into the line.

10. Relief complete will be sent to Bn HQ by wire. Code Word:- "SEA BREEZE"

11. Acknowledge.

(Signed) E.C.S. JOHNSON
2/Lieut & a/adjutant
2/4th Bn Gloster Regt.

Copy No. 1   War Diary
    2+3   O.C. Coys.
    4   Q.M. & T.O.
    5   R.S.M.
    6   183 Inf. Bde.
    7   2nd R.M. Bn.
    8   ANSON Bn.
    9   File.

7/4th Gloster Regt

OPERATION ORDERS No 104
By Lt Col DG Bayley Commdg   Secret

Ref 57c.   Copy No 6

1. 7/4 Glosters will march tomorrow to billets
in ETRICOURT - MANANCOURT area.

2. Route MEZ - FINS - EQUANCOURT.
Order of march - HQ - No 1 Coy - No 2 Coy
Distances of 200x will be maintained
between platoons
HQ will move off at ZERO hour -
Zero hour will be communicated to
all concerned as soon as possible.
Transport will move behind the
Battalion.

3. QM will send 2 cookers to new
area tomorrow morning. Dinners
will be cooked in these and eaten on
arrival of the Battalion.
QM will be responsible for
billeting in new area and will
arrange guides at Eastern exit
from ETRICOURT.

4. 3 Baggage wagons will arrive at
the camp about 9am for conveyance
of blankets, officers kits and mess

baskets. Blankets will be rolled and carried together with officers kits and the baskets. By Zero less 1 hour O.C. "A" Coy will detail a loading party of 1 Sergeant and 8 men.

5. Transport and Q.M. stores will remain at EQUANCOURT. Transport Officer will arrange for 4 Lewis Gun limbers to be at new camp at 3pm tomorrow. O.C. Coys will arrange that all Lewis Gun equipment is ready for loading at the above time. Limbers will go to Transport lines after being loaded.

6. On the 24th inst. the Battalion less marching portion of Transport will entrain at ETRICOURT and move by rail to the BRAY-SUR-SOMME area. Detraining station - BUIRE. H.Q.'s will be billeted at BRAY.

Capt R.L. VERNON and 3 O.R.'s (with 2 bicycles) detailed by Q.M. will meet the Staff Captain at 9am tomorrow at EQUANCOURT x rds and proceed in advance to new area. Separate orders have been issued to Capt Vernon.

7. ACKNOWLEDGE
Issued at 4pm.

Addendum to O/O No 10%   SECRET

22/12/17

1. Steel helmets will not be worn on the march.

2. Starting point will be the Southern exit of the wood Q.15.c.1.8. H.Q. will pass the starting point at 10.35 a.m. O.C. Coys will arrange their times accordingly.

3. 200 yds distance between Coys and every eight vehicles will be maintained.

4. Blankets: officers kits and mess baskets will be dumped at Bn H.Q. by 9 a.m.

S.J. Stotesbury
Capt & adj
2/4/ London

22/12/17

2/4th Battalion Gloucestershire Regiment.

S E C R E T.   OPERATION ORDERS No. 105.   COPY No. 1.

By Lieut.Colonel D.G.BAYNSLEY, Comdg.   In the Field, 23.12.17.

Ref. 57C 1/40,000.
AMIENS 1/10,000.

1. 2/4th Glosters will move tomorrow by road and rail to BRAY-SUR-SOMME in accordance with tables "A" & "B" attached.

2. Transport less vehicles and personnel shown in table "B" will proceed by road. Separate orders have been issued to the Transport officer.

3. The Battalion will detrain at BUIRE where guides will meet and conduct to billets in BRAY.

4. Lieut. Page will be in charge of personnel, horses and vehicles detailed in table "B". Lieut. Page will arrange starting time for vehicles, horses and accompanying personnel.
   The officer and 100 O.R. shown in table "B" will be found by No. 2 Coy.. Party will march off from the camp at 5 p.m. 2/Lieut. Giles will be in charge.

5. All Transport will arrive two hours before and personnel one hour before departure of the train. Transport officer will provide drag ropes for use as breast-lines in the trucks.

6. Dress for the march:- S.D. caps - leather jerkins will be worn. Two lorries will be available for carrying blankets etc. Blankets will be rolled and dumped in Coy. dumps Battn.T.Q. by 8.45 a.m. Officers' valises and mess baskets will be dumped at the same place and hour. Each Coy. will detail a loading party of 1 Sergt. and 6 O.R.
   One lorry will be at the disposal of the Q.M. for carrying surplus stores. Lorry will report at EQUANCOURT x rds. at 8 a.m. Q.M. will be responsible for returning lorries to their park with written instructions immediately they are unloaded.

7. **Supply Arrangements.**
   Supply wagons have moved to new area in advance of the Brigade group. Refilling on the 24th will be on arrival and on the following days at 9.0 a.m.
   Refilling Point:- 1 km W. of BRAY on BRAY - CORBIE roads.
   Fuel Dump:-   at R.P.

8. The greatest care will be taken to leave all billets clean. Certificates that billets at EQUANCOURT have been left clean will be obtained by the Q.M. and Transport Officer from the Area Commandant of EQUANCOURT.
   2/Lieut. Grose will meet the Area Commandant's representative at 11.30 a.m., on the road opposite the Northumberland Hussars Camp, for the purpose of receiving clean billet certificates.

10. O.C.No.1 Coy. will arrange for 20 shovels to be carried on the train for use in case of emergency.

11. Falling out states and location reports will be rendered immediately on arrival.

12. ACKNOWLEDGE.

                                    (Signed) S.J.STOTESBURY.
                                        Captain & Adjutant.
Issued at 11 p.m.   2/4th Gloucestershires.

        Copies to:-
                No.1   War Diary.
                   2   C.O.
                 3-4   O.C.Coys.
                   5   183rd Inf. Bde.
                   6   R.S.M.
                   7   Q.M. & T.O.
                   8   File
                   9   Spare.

2/4th Battalion Gloucestershire Regiment.

BATTALION ORDERS No.100.

By Lieut.Colonel ...., Commanding.   In the Field, 31.12.17.

Ref: Maps 1/100,000.

1. 2/4th Glosters will move tomorrow by road to GUILLAUCOURT.

2. **Starting Point:-** BRAY Square.

   Route:- FRICOURT - ....

   Order of March: Bn.H.q., "A","B","C","D" Coys., Transport.
   ..... will pass the starting point at ....a.m. There will be no
   interval between Coys. Interval of 200 yards will be maintained
   between groups of 10 wagons. There will be an interval of 50 yards
   between the rear of the Battalion and the head of the Transport.
   Two sections of "A" Coy. and Battalion Pioneers will march in front
   of the Transport to sprinkle earth and stones on the roads where
   particularly slippery. Tools for this purpose will be obtained from
   tool limbers which will be in front of the Transport instead of in
   the normal position. One section of "D" Coy. will march in rear of
   each group of 10 wagons to assist wagons up hills and in bad places,
   if necessary with drag ropes.
      The Battalion Police will march in rear of the Transport under the
   Orderly Officer and act as rear-guard.
      Muleteers will report to the Transport Officer at 8.0 p.m. tonight.

3. Blankets, officers' kits and mess baskets will be conveyed by lorry
   and will be dumped outside "A" and "B" Company billets by 8.0 a.m.
   H.Q. Blankets etc. will be dumped outside Bttn.H.q. by the same hour.

4. Three lorries will be at Bde.H.q. at 9.0 a.m. Quartermaster
   will arrange for guides.

5. **Rations.**

Date.	Location.	Time.
31st Dec.	Half way between GUILLAUCOURT and .... on south side of road.	About 12 noon.
1st Jan. & in future.	ditto.	9.0 a.m.

   Fuel dump at .... CHURCH.
   Ordnance Stores and Mob. Veterinary Section will be at ....

6. Billets will be left perfectly clean and will be ready for
   inspection by Major Wyatt and M.O. by 7.45 a.m.

7. Falling-out States and location reports will be rendered immediately
   on arrival in new billets.

8. Dinners will be on arrival in new billets.

9. ....

                              (Signed) .... ,
                                Captain & Adjutant.
Issued at .8.30.p.m.   2/4th Battn. Gloucester Regt.

   Copies to:-

   No.1   C.O.
      2   War Diary.
      3-6 O.C. Coys.
      7   Q.M.
      8   T.O.
      9   R.S.M.
     10   183rd Inf. Bde.
     11   File.

TABLE A

Last train starting 11am from ETRICOURT STN.

Serial No.	Unit	S.P.	Time	From	To
1	Bn HQ	Bn HQ	11.52 am	MANANCOURT	BRAY.
2	No 1 Coy.	ditto	11.53 am	" —	" —
3	No 2 Coy (less 1 off & 100 OR)	ditto	11.54 am	" —	" —

NOTE:- Billets in new area may have to be changed but guides will know route.

TABLE B.

Third (Omnibus) train starting at 8 p.m. from YTRES STN

	Personnel Off.	O.R.	Horses.	4 Wheeled Vehicles.	2 Wheeled Vehicles.
H. Cookers		8	8	4	
Maltese Cart		2	1		1
Water Carts		2	2	1	2
Mess Cart		1	1	1	
Chargers	1		8	1	1
O.R.	1	100	1	1	1

All personnel and vehicles will arrive at YTRES Station by 6 p.m. O.C. No.2 Coy will detail a party of 1 Off. + 50 O.R. from men going in this train to report to Capt. HARNET at YTRES station at 6 p.m. for loading vehicles.

www.ingramcontent.com/pod-product-compliance
Lightning Source LLC
Chambersburg PA
CBHW081356160426
43192CB00013B/2424